T0104131

TOP **10**
COPENHAGEN

Top 10 Copenhagen Highlights

The Top 10 of Everything

CONTENTS

Copenhagen Area by Area

Streetsmart

Within each Top 10 list in this book, no hierarchy of quality or popularity is implied. All 10 are, in the editor's opinion, of roughly equal merit.

Title page, front cover and spine
Canal houses and boats along Nyhavn
Back cover, clockwise from top left
A traditional Danish sandwich;
Amagertorv town square; the scenic
Frederiksborg Slot; Nyhavn waterfront
houses; sunset in the Old Town

The rapid rate at which the world is changing is constantly keeping the DK Eyewitness team on our toes. While we've worked hard to ensure that this edition of Copenhagen is accurate and up-to-date, we know that opening hours alter, standards shift, prices fluctuate, places close and new ones pop up in their stead. So, if you notice we've got something wrong or left something out, we want to hear about it. Please get in touch at **travelguides@dk.com**

Welcome to
Copenhagen

With its superlative restaurants, design-led stores and wealth of art galleries, Copenhagen is the cultural capital of northern Europe as well as one of the world's most liveable cities. A place where opulent palaces stand shoulder to shoulder with modern architectural masterpieces, the Danish capital can be experienced in a multitude of ways. With DK Eyewitness Top 10 Copenhagen, it's yours to explore.

Copenhagen has royal credentials that are clear the moment you set foot on the city's cobblestone streets, with magnificent palaces, castles and churches dominating the skyline. But even with its regal past (it's home to the world's oldest monarchy) casting a long shadow, Copenhagen remains a dynamic, modern city with much to offer to even the most museum-wary traveller. Here, world-class restaurants serve groundbreaking dishes, high-end boutiques sell sustainable goodies and breathtaking parks offer a retreat from the urban buzz.

It's no coincidence that Denmark is often cited as the happiest nation on earth. Danes may be direct – and their humour dry – but they know better than most how to enjoy the finer things in life. After all, hygge – the Danish lifestyle trend that loosely translates into a feeling of warmth and cosiness – is now almost as popular outside of Denmark as one of the country's other great exports: beer.

Whether you're visiting for a weekend or a week, our Top 10 guide brings together the best of everything the city has to offer, from vibrant **Vesterbro** to stately **Slotsholmen** and beyond. The guide has useful tips throughout, from seeking out what's free to places off the beaten track, plus seven easy-to-follow itineraries, designed to tie together a clutch of sights in a short space of time. Add inspiring photography and detailed maps, and you've got the essential pocket-sized travel companion. **Enjoy the book, and enjoy Copenhagen**.

Clockwise from top: **Christiansborg Slot, the interior of Grundtvigs Kirke, houses on Nyhavn, Frederiksborg Slot, ceiling of Marmorkirken dome, Amalienborg sentries, street art in Christiania**

Exploring Copenhagen

Copenhagen may not be the biggest of capital cities, but it punches well above its weight in terms of culture, history and charm. Despite its compact size, there is a lot to see and do. To help you make the most of your visit, here are some ideas for a two- or four-day trip.

Christiansborg Slot has magnificent interiors.

Key
— Two-day itinerary
— Four-day itinerary

Nyhavn is a waterfront entertainment area.

Frederiksberg Have
Elephant Viewpoint
Pile Alle
Vesterbrogade
Bakkehuset
Visit Carlsberg
Kødby
Sønder Boulevard

Two Days in Copenhagen

Day ❶
MORNING
Set sail from **Nyhavn** (see pp22–3) on a canal tour, then stroll along the promenade past the Royal Danish Playhouse. Follow the harbourside path until you reach **Amalienborg** (see pp24–5), where you can watch the changing of the guard. Have lunch at **Kompasset** (see p75).

AFTERNOON
Head west on Gothersgade until you reach **Kongens Have** (see pp16–17). Stroll through the gardens, then continue to **Rosenborg Slot** (see pp16–17) to see the crown jewels. Walk north on Øster Voldgade and visit **SMK – National Gallery of Denmark** (see pp26–7), ending the afternoon with a drink at **Torvehallerne KBH** (see p63).

Day ❷
MORNING
Begin the day at **Nationalmuseet** (see pp32–3), making sure to visit the Viking exhibition. Next, go to **Slotsholmen** (see pp30–31) and visit the Royal Stables before taking a tour of the Royal Reception Rooms at Christiansborg Slot. For an innovative spin on a *smørrebrød* (open sandwich), stop at the Tower Restaurant.

AFTERNOON
Head southwest on Stormgade to **Ny Carlsberg Glyptotek** (see p70), before crossing Tietgensgade and exploring **Tivoli** (see pp14–15). After spending a couple of hours here, exit onto Vesterbrogade and walk east towards the **Latin Quarter** (see pp18–19) for sightseeing and shopping.

Four Days in Copenhagen

Day ❶
MORNING
Make **SMK – National Gallery of Denmark** (see pp26–7) your first stop of the day, then cross Georg Brandes Plads and head to **Rosenborg Slot** (see pp16–17). Take a guided tour of the 17th-century palace before exiting

Day ❸

MORNING

Start the day with a stroll through **Frederiksberg Have** (see p87), pausing at the Elephant Viewpoint overlooking the zoo's Elephant House before exiting onto Pile Alle. Pass under the elephant gate and make your way into **Visit Carlsberg** (see p88).

AFTERNOON

Stroll northeast and stop at **Bakkehuset** (see p89). Turn right to get onto Vesterbrogade and call in at **Sønder Boulevard** (see p89) for a late lunch. Continue on Vesterbrogade and turn right onto Gasværksvej, following the road until you reach Kødbyen's trendy bars.

into **Kongens Have** (see pp16–17). Head east to **Marmorkirken**, and then on to **Amalienborg** (see pp24–5). Stop at **Orangeriet Kongens Have** (see p83) for a hearty meal.

AFTERNOON

Walk west, stopping to admire the Gefionspringvandet and St Alban's Church before crossing the footbridge into **Kastellet** (see p80). See the **Little Mermaid** (see p80) from the fortress ramparts, then catch a 1A bus into **Kongens Nytorv** (see pp22–3). Stroll along Strøget and later, sit for a drink at one of Amagertorv's cafés.

Day ❷

MORNING

Start the day at **Nationalmuseet** (see pp32–3) and museum-hop on **Slotsholmen** (see pp30–31) before popping into the Royal Stables. Take a torchlit tour of the ruins under Christiansborg Slot.

AFTERNOON

Cross the **harbour** (see pp12–13) and enter Christianshavn. Turn right to visit the **Christians Kirke** (see p93) on Strandgade, then head east until you reach the canal, crossing the bridge on Sankt Annæ Gade and arrive at **Vor Frelsers Kirke** (see p94). Spend the afternoon in **Christiania** (see pp28–9).

Day ❹

MORNING

Begin the day with a coffee at one of the many cafés along Studiestræde before exploring the bustling **Latin Quarter** (see pp18–19). Head up Store Kannikestræde to Rundetaarn, and then hike to the top. Continue into **Nyhavn** (see pp22–3) for lunch.

AFTERNOON

Take a boat tour of the canals and hop off at **Holmens Kirke** (see p41). Walk west along Gammel Strand, passing **Rådhus** (see p70) before turning onto Vesterbrogade. Take a left into **Tivoli** (see pp14–15), and spend the afternoon wandering the beautiful 19th-century pleasure gardens.

Tivoli's exclusive boutique hotel in a charming fairy-tale setting.

Top 10 Copenhagen Highlights

Fishing boats on the water in the historic district of Nyhavn

TOP 10 Copenhagen Highlights

Copenhagen is a vibrant city offering an array of experiences. Walk through the cobbled streets of the medieval centre, explore world-class museums, experience the finest restaurants and hippest nightlife, or simply unwind beside the gorgeous waters of one of the nearby peaceful seaside towns. This charming destination has something for everyone.

1 Harbour Sights

The best way to soak up Copenhagen's harbour sights is to take a boat trip along the canals of Slotsholmen and Christianshavn. It is also a good way to understand the city's development (see pp12–13).

2 Tivoli

This pleasure garden and fun-fair attracts both kids and adults. The rides are great for an adrenaline rush, and if you feel peckish there are many restaurants (see pp14–15).

3 Rosenborg Slot and Kongens Have

Set in one of the city's prettiest parks, the lovely 17th-century Rosenborg Castle houses the royal regalia, including the dazzling Crown Jewels (see pp16–17).

4 Latin Quarter

One of the oldest areas in Copenhagen, the Latin Quarter is just off the main pedestrianized street, Strøget (see pp18–19).

5 Kongens Nytorv and Nyhavn

Kongens Nytorv (King's New Square) is a splendid Baroque square at the top of Nyhavn. Previously a seedy haunt for sailors, Nyhavn has been radically transformed. It is now a waterside attraction with bars and restaurants (see pp22–3).

6 Amalienborg and Frederiksstaden

Home to the royal family since 1794, this complex of palaces represents some of the best Rococo architecture in Denmark, plus fascinating displays *(see pp24–5)*.

7 SMK – National Gallery of Denmark

You will find a wonderful collection of Danish and European sculpture as well as paintings at the SMK. It is housed in a beautiful 19th-century building, connected by a glass bridge to a modern wing *(see pp26–7)*.

8 Christiania

A wonderland of cafés, bars, music venues, art galleries and fiercely independent shops – Christiania is a must-see for anyone interested in the city's thriving counter-culture *(see pp28–9)*.

10 Nationalmuseet

Here is a perfect example of how brilliantly the Danes design their museums. You will find some fabulous ethnographic artifacts from around the world, as well as an excellent children's museum *(see pp32–3)*.

9 Slotsholmen

This is where it all began in the 12th century. The present Neo-Baroque castle was built in 1907–28, but was never inhabited by the monarch. It is shared between the royals and Parliament *(see pp30–31)*.

Harbour Sights

A harbour tour is a delightful way to take in the city's brilliant views and varied topography. You will be taken along the wide waters of the Inner Harbour and winding waterways of Christianshavn, then round to Slotsholmen (the island on which the original town of Havn flourished in the 12th century). Vor Frelsers Kirke, in particular, makes a spectacular sight as you look up through the rigging of sailing boats dotting the Christianshavn canal.

1 The Canals
You can glide along on the canals **(above)** during a tour. These were built in a Dutch style in 1618 at the command of Christian IV. It is because of this that Christianshavn is known as "Little Amsterdam".

2 Operaen
The Opera House **(below)** was built in just four years. Its massive, orange-maple coloured auditorium *(see pp94–5)* seats 1,700 people. The foyer's sculptures change colour with the weather.

3 Vor Frelsers Kirke
With a soaring twisted spire, this opulent church dominates the Christianshavn skyline. An ascent offers an unparalleled vantage point over the city.

4 Nyhavn
Even today, the utterly charming old harbour of Nyhavn *(see p22)* is filled with boats. The old brothels and pubs have now been turned into respectable bars and restaurants serving good, traditional Danish dishes.

5 Den Sorte Diamant
The Black Diamond is a vast, eye-catching structure that holds all the books ever published in Denmark. It is the largest library *(see p64)* in the Nordic countries, and is a wonderful place to find original Danish texts.

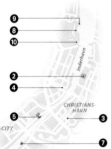

7 Havnebadet
Take a refreshing dip in the sparkling clean harbour waters **(left)** of this popular open-air pool *(see p49)*, while enjoying superb views of the city. There are three pools to choose from – for adults, for children and a smaller pool for divers.

8 Langelinie
One of the city's most scenic areas, this is a wonderful place to walk along the harbour banks. Stroll along, past Kastellet and the *Little Mermaid*, right up to the final stretch where there is a cruise ship terminal.

9 The Little Mermaid
Den Lille Havfrue *(see p80)* is a surprisingly small landmark, ordered by brewery magnate Carl Jacobsen in 1909 as a gift to the city of Copenhagen. It was created in 1913 by Edvard Eriksen, who modelled the sculpture after his wife Eline.

10 Pavilions and the Royal Yacht
On the quayside, just beyond the *Little Mermaid*, are two green-domed pavilions. It is here that the Danish royal family gathers before boarding their stunning 79-m (259-ft) royal yacht, called the *Dannebrog* **(right)**, which shares its name with the Danish flag (said to have fallen from the sky in the year 1219).

> **MUTANT MERMAID**
>
> Set close to the *Little Mermaid*, and almost inviting controversy, is a sculpture group called *Paradise Genetically Altered* by Danish artist Bjørn Nørgaard. There is a triumphal arch, with a 9-m (29-ft) genetically altered Madonna atop it, surrounded by figures of Adam, Eve, Christ, Mary Magdalene, the Tripartite Capital – a critical representation of capitalism – and a pregnant man. On its own small island not far away sits the *Genetically Modified Little Mermaid*.

Harbour Sights

6 Houseboats
Along the canals the houseboats range from boat-like structures to some with barge-like designs, and other homes built on floating plat-forms, complete with outdoor spaces.

NEED TO KNOW

MAP L4

■ Both Stromma and Netto Boats offer guided canal and harbour tours *(see p109)*.

■ The tours run daily round the year, with several departures per day.

■ Public harbour buses 991 and 992 run from Refsahaleøen, Holmen, Operan, Nyhavn, and Den Sorte Diamant. Bus 993 connects Refshaleøen and Nyhavn.

■ Harbour buses use the same ticket or cards valid for other modes of trans-port. Copenhagen Cards *(see p112)* are accepted.

TOP 10 ⭐ Tivoli

Famous for its fairy-tale ambience, eye-catching buildings, gorgeous landscaped gardens and upmarket entertainment and restaurants, Tivoli Gardens are more than an amusement park. The atmosphere is magical enough to merit a visit even if you are not interested in the excellent rides on offer. Founded in 1843, Tivoli has long been a favourite with royalty. It also proved to be a great source of inspiration for Walt Disney, who visited in the 1950s and is said to have been fascinated by Tivoli's ambience.

2 Thrill Rides

Day or night, Tivoli rings with the shrieks of visitors whizzing along on thrill rides such as Aquila, The Demon **(left)**, Vertigo and The Starflyer, which reaches a height of 80 m (262 ft).

1 Gentle Rides

For children and adults who are not keen on thrill rides, there are plenty of gentle options. The Ferris wheel is an observation wheel that offers great views over Tivoli. You could also enjoy a trolley-bus ride, a carousel ride with music, a waltzer in the shape of a pirate ship and several kids' rides, such as flying dragons and miniature classic cars.

3 Tivoli Concert Hall and Open-Air Stage

The hall hosts varied performances. There are free rock concerts on Friday nights (May–Sep), which often feature renowned artists.

4 Pantomime Theatre

Built in 1874, this theatre **(below)** has an elaborate Chinese design and a spectacular stage curtain styled like a peacock's tail. It is known for its enjoyable mime shows.

5 Dragon Boats

These boats **(above)** are very popular rides at Tivoli. Kids love floating on the lake during the day. In the evenings, the setting turns romantic.

6 Tivoli at Night

At night Tivoli is utterly magical, sparkling resplendently with thousands of fairy lights and Chinese lanterns. You can catch the dazzling Tivoli Illuminations over the lake and an exuberant late-night show with fireworks, lasers, music and waterjets.

7 Traditional Rides

Tivoli's current Ferris wheel dates from 1943. The Roller Coaster **(left)** was built in 1914 and is one of the oldest of its kind. It reaches speeds of 58 kmph (36 mph). The classic carousel is also very popular, perfect for adults looking for a dose of nostalgia.

9 Tivoli Akvarium

Don't miss the amazing aquarium in the foyer of the Concert Hall. Modelled on a tropical coral reef, this extensive saltwater aquarium is home to more than 1,600 fish of over 500 varieties. Among the popular attractions are the eels.

10 Tivoli Youth Guard

A tradition since 1844, the Youth Guard parades through Tivoli – complete with instruments, coach and horses – forming a delightful picture.

NEED TO KNOW

MAP H5

■ Vesterbrogade 3 ■ 33 15 10 01 ■ www.tivoli.dk

Open hours vary; check website for details

Adm (charges may vary; check website for details)

■ Go on the thrill rides during the day, as long queues can build up in the evenings.

■ In the Bernstorffsgade corner of the gardens, the Foodhall offers an innovative spin on haute cuisine.

8 Nimb Hotel

This splendid hotel **(below)**, housed in the Nimb building, offers a variety of culinary experiences, such as Nimb Brasserie, the Cakenhagen (bakery), a Bar'n'Grill with delicacies from the grill.

TOP 10 ★ Rosenborg Slot and Kongens Have

Rosenborg Castle had originally been built as a summer house between 1606 and 1632 by Christian IV. At that time, it stood surrounded by sprawling gardens (now the Kongens Have park). This was Christian IV's favourite castle, and many rooms retain the original Renaissance decor from his residency. When he was on his deathbed at Frederiksborg Castle in 1648, he insisted on being brought to Rosenborg Castle, and eventually died here.

1 Knight's Hall
Known as the Long Hall before 1750, this room (above) was completed in 1624 as a celebration hall. Only two Dutch fireplaces still remain from its original elaborate decorations.

3 Marble Hall
Originally serving as the bedroom of Kirsten Munk, Christian IV's morganatic wife, this room was turned into a Baroque show of splendour to celebrate the Absolute Monarchy.

2 Royal Residence
Complete with fairy-tale turrets and bronze lions guarding the entrance (below), the castle is wholly regal. In 1838, it became the first royal residence to be opened to the public.

4 Crown Jewels
The castle has been used as the treasury of the realm since 1658. In the castle's heavily guarded basement are Denmark's Crown Jewels (above).

5 Dark Room
This room is filled with fascinating objects, such as wax portraits of Frederik III and a 17th-century trick chair.

ROSENBORG'S KINGS

Christian IV: Built many Renaissance buildings.
Frederik III: Introduced Absolute Monarchy to control the aristocracy.
Christian V: Introduced fair taxation.
Frederik IV: Constructed Frederiksberg Castle.
Christian VI: Known as the religious king.
Frederik V: Responsible for the building of the Frederiksstaden district.

8 Frederik IV's Chamber Room

In the 1700s, this room **(above)** was used by Frederik IV's sister as an antechamber and the tapestries that hang here date back to this period. Note the intricate equestrian silver statue of Frederik. The coffered ceiling is the original.

9 Christian IV's Bedroom

Another private royal apartment, this room contains Christian IV's bloodied clothing, from the naval battle of Kolberger Heide (1644) where he lost an eye. The king wanted these clothes preserved as national mementos.

10 Winter Room

This panelled room **(below)** is said to have been one of Christian IV's most important private chambers. Look out for the speaking tubes that connect with the wine cellar and room above.

6 Glass Cabinet

This room was designed as a glass cabinet in 1713–14 by Frederik IV. The cabinet was built to house the extensive collection of glassware presented to Frederik in 1709 by the city of Venice, and it's contents are amazing.

7 Kongens Have

Visited by over two million people every year, Denmark's oldest royal gardens date back to the 17th century. The rose garden here contains many wonderful statues. Various art events and a puppet theatre for children are organized during summer.

NEED TO KNOW

MAP J2 ■ Øster Voldgade 4A ■ 33 15 32 86 ■ www.rosenborgslot.dk

Open hours vary; check website for details

Adm 123 Dkr, students 80 Dkr, under-18s free; Copenhagen Card accepted

■ Rosenborg Slot is a short walk away from the official Danish royal palace, Amalienborg Slot.

■ Guided tours (60–90 minutes long) are available in English, German and French (advance booking is required).

■ Entry to the Kongens Have is free for all.

■ Avoid lurking near the guards at the entrance to the Crown Jewels.

■ Browse through items inspired by Royal Danish history at the gift shop.

TOP 10 ⭐ Latin Quarter

The Latin Quarter is home to Copenhagen's university, where Latin used to be the spoken language. One of the oldest areas in the city, it is full of 17th-century buildings that were built by the architect king, Christian IV. Although there have been dwellings here since medieval times, most of them were destroyed in the disastrous fire that spread across Copenhagen in 1728. Today, the Latin Quarter is a lively and bustling student area brimming with shops and cafés.

Højbro Plads ①
This cobbled square **(right)** is located close to the canal. There, under the Hojbro bridge, can be found Agnete and the Merman, an underwater statue by the Danish artist Suste Bonnén.

② Sankt Petri Kirke
Older than Vor Frue Kirke, Copenhagen's German church *(see p39)* also suffered from city fires and the British bombardment of 1807. Its vaulted sepulchral chapel has monuments and tombs dating back to 1681.

Latin Quarter

⑤ Rundetaarn
The Round Tower *(see p46)* was built in 1642 by Christian IV as an observatory, its official role until 1861. It is 34.8 m (114 ft) high, with an internal ramp that spirals almost to the top. It holds art exhibitions and concerts in the library hall.

③ Regensen
This 17th-century student residence lies opposite the Rundetaarn. A part of it burned down in the great fire of 1728, but was soon rebuilt. Its students retain the old tradition of "storming" Rundetaarn every May.

④ Gråbrødretorv
Named after the Grey Brothers who built Copenhagen's first monastery here, this lovely 13th-century square **(right)** is now a popular place for locals and visitors to enjoy alfresco meals or drinks.

7 Trinitatis Kirke

This magnificent church (left) was built in 1637–56 for the staff and students of the university. If the church (see p38) happens to be closed when you visit, you can enter Rundetaarn and get a view of the church nave through the glass panel at the start of the ramp.

8 Universitetet

Founded in 1479 by Christian I, the University of Copenhagen was the country's first university. The Neo-Classical building that can be seen here today dates to the 19th century. In the courtyard, lie the remains of an old Bishop's Palace (1420). Most of the university's campus is now on the island of Amager.

THE BELLS AND CARILLON OF HELLIGÅNDSKIRKEN

In 1647, 50 years after the clock tower was built, king Christian IV gifted the church a set of bells and a carillon. The carillon consisted of 19 bells. It was also used at funerals; the importance of the deceased decided for how long the bells would chime – sometimes hours.

10 Vor Frue Kirke

In the 12th century, Bishop Absalon founded a Gothic church (see p39) here. After burning down twice, the current-standing Neo-Classical cathedral (below), as well as the tower, were completed in 1829.

6 Synagogen

Built between 1830 and 1833, Copenhagen's oldest synagogue survived Nazi occupation. The synagogue has Egyptian elements in the columns, ceiling and the cornice over the arc.

9 Helligåndskirken

The Church of the Holy Ghost (see p39) was built in 1295 as a hospital for the weak and elderly, and was expanded to include a monastery in 1474.

NEED TO KNOW
MAP J4

Sankt Petri Kirke: Skt Peders St 2; 33 13 38 33; open 11am–3pm Tue–Sat; adm (sepulchral chapel); www.sankt-petri.dk

Rundetaarn: Købmagergade 52A; 33 73 03 73; open Apr–Sep: 10am–8pm daily, Oct–Mar: 10am–6pm Mon, Thu–Sun, 10am–9pm Tue–Wed; adm 40 Dkr (10 Dkr for 5–10 year olds); free with Copenhagen Card; www.rundetaarn.dk

Synagogen: Krystalgade 12; 33 12 88 68; open 9am–noon Mon & Wed, 10am–noon Tue, 1–4pm Thu

Vor Frue Kirke: Nørregade 8; open 8am–5pm Mon–Sat

Trinitatis Kirke: Købmagergade 52A; open 9:30am–4:30pm Mon–Fri; www.trinitatiskirke.dk

Universitetet: Nørregade 10; 35 32 26 26; open 8am–9pm Mon–Thu, 8am–6pm Fri; www.ku.dk

Hellingåndskirken: Niels Hemmingsens Gade 5; 33 15 41 44; open noon–4pm Mon–Fri, 11am–1pm Sat; www.helligaandskirken.dk

Following pages Statue of Frederik V and Marmorkirken, Amalienborg

🔟⭐ Kongens Nytorv and Nyhavn

Kongens Nytorv (the King's New Square) and Nyhavn (New Harbour) are two of the most picturesque areas in Copenhagen. Nearly 300 years old, Kongens Nytorv is where Det Kongelige Teater (the Royal Theatre) and Charlottenborg Slot are located. The square was once outside the city gates and the site of the town gallows. The Nyhavn canal was planned by Frederik III to connect the Inner Harbour with the square, enabling merchants to unload their goods.

1 Nyhavn Nos 18, 20 and 67

These brightly painted merchants' houses *(see p47)* were built together with the harbour. Fairy-tale writer Hans Christian Andersen lived in them – he wrote the fairy tale, *The Tinder Box* (1835), while living at No 20.

2 Nyhavn Canal

Running down to the Inner Harbour, this canal **(right)** is flanked by houses that belonged to merchants. A large anchor, installed in honour of the sailors who lost their lives in World War II, marks the starting point of Nyhavn.

Kongens Nytorv and Nyhavn

3 Charlottenborg Slot

An early example of the Danish Baroque style, this palace was built by Frederik III's son Ulrik. It houses the Royal Danish Academy of Fine Arts as well as the Kunsthal Charlottenborg.

4 Hotel d'Angleterre

This is Copenhagen's oldest hotel **(below)** and one of the oldest in the world *(see p114)*. It has hosted many personalities such as Karen Blixen, Winston Churchill, Grace Kelly and Madonna.

5 Magasin du Nord

Originally the famous Hotel du Nord, this is Copenhagen's oldest department store and is considered to be the city's answer to London's Selfridges or New York's Bloomingdale's.

6 Amber Museum

Set in a house dating back to 1606, this small museum displays an exquisite collection dedicated to Denmark's national gem, amber (also called Nordic Gold).

8 Equestrian Statue

The bronze statue **(left)** in the middle of Kongens Nytorv commemorates Christian V (1646–99), who rebuilt the square in 1670 in Baroque style. Created by the French-born court sculptor Abraham-César Lamoureux, it shows the king dressed as a Roman emperor.

"THE IMPERIAL ETHIOPIAN PALACE"

In the 1950s, Ethopia's emperor Haile Selassie, with his family and entourage, visited Denmark and stayed at the Hotel d'Angleterre. During their stay, all telephone calls to the hotel were answered with "The Imperial Ethiopian Palace".

9 Store Strandstræde and Lille Strandstræde

Once full of brothels and pubs, "Big Beach Street" and "Little Beach Street" are now home to art galleries and stylish designer shops.

10 Det Kongelige Teater

This Baroque-style theatre is home to the Royal Danish Ballet **(below)** and is the third one to stand on this site.

7 Vingårdsstræde 6

At the age of 22, Hans Christian Andersen lived for a year in the attic of this building *(see p46)*, one of the city's oldest, built on the site of a vineyard (hence *Vingårdsstræde*). Its 13th-century cellars now host the Michelin-starred Kong Hans Kælder *(see p75)*.

NEED TO KNOW

MAP K4–L4

Charlottenborg Slot: Nyhavn 2; 33 74 46 39; open noon–8pm Tue–Fri, 11am–5pm Sat–Sun; adm 90 Dkr, under-15s free, students 50 Dkr, free after 5pm Wed; www.kunsthal charlottenborg.dk

Magasin du Nord: Kongens Nytorv 13; open 10am–8pm daily; www.magasin.dk

Amber Museum: Kongens Nytorv 2; 39 55 08 00; open 10am–5pm Mon–Fri (from 11am Sat); adm 25 Dkr (under-15s free); www. houseofamber.com

Det Kongelige Teater: Kongens Nytorv; 33 69 69 33;

guided tours available, book at the box office or in advance; www.kglteater.dk

■ The restaurants on the south side of Nyhavn are good and usually not as busy as those on the north.

■ To find a quick bite away from the crowds in Nyhavn, stop by Pizzeria at 8 Lille Strandstræde.

TOP 10 ★ Amalienborg and Frederiksstaden

Built in the 1750s, this stately complex was designed by the royal architect, Nicolai Eigtved. Four Rococo palaces, originally home to four noble families, enclose an octagonal square in Frederiksstaden, an aristocratic area built by Frederik V. Christian VII bought the palaces after the Christiansborg Slot burned down in 1794, and the royal family has lived here ever since. It was named after a palace built on this site by Queen Sophie Amalie in the 17th century.

Christian VII's Palace ❶

This palace **(right)** was one of the first to be completed by the time of Eigtved's death in 1754. Also known as Moltke Palace – named after its original owner, Count Adam Gottlob Moltke – it is the most expensive palace in the complex and also has one of the best Rococo interiors in the entire country.

❸ Frederik VIII's Palace

This palace, which has a clock on its façade, was renamed after Frederik VIII moved in. It is now the residence of Crown Prince Frederik and Crown Princess Mary.

❺ The Golden Axis

Marmorkirken and Frederiksstaden lie on a short axis called the Golden Axis, which was considered very important when the Opera House was built.

❹ Amaliehaven

The Amalie Garden was created in 1983 on the banks of the Harbour, financed by the shipping giant A P Møller and the Christine McKinney Møller Foundation. It has a splendid fountain.

❷ Palace Guards

When the queen is in residence, the Danish Royal Life Guards **(above)** stand outside the palace, guarding their monarch in two-hour shifts. At noon, guards from Rosenborg Slot take over, marching through the city streets just before noon.

NEED TO KNOW

MAP L3

Marmorkirken: Frederiksgade 4; 33 91 27 06; open 10am–5pm Mon–Thu & Sat, noon–5pm Fri & Sun; adm; www.marmor kirken.dk

Amalienborg Museum: 33 15 32 86; open late Jan–late Oct: 10am–5pm daily; late Oct–Dec: 11am–4pm Tue–Sun; adm 125 Dkr, under-18s free, students 80 Dkr, free with Copenhagen Card; www.dkks.dk

■ **Guided tours of Christian VII's palace can be booked online or at the ticket office.**

■ **Avoid sitting on palace steps.**

■ **Amaliehaven is right next to Nyhavn and is a popular place for a walk.**

THE RUSSIAN CONNECTION

The onion domes of Alexander Nevsky Kirke, the Russian Orthodox Church, are easy to identify. Consecrated in 1883, it was a gift from Tsar Alexander III to mark his marriage to the Danish Princess Marie Dagmar in 1866.

9 Colonnade

Caspar Harsdorff, Christian VII's architect, built this Classical-style colonnade between 1794 and 1795. Supported by eight ionic columns, it connects two palaces.

10 Christian IX's Palace

The first royal family to live here was Crown Prince Frederik VI's (1794). Since 1967, it has been home to the Queen and Prince Consort Henrik.

6 Marmorkirken

Properly called Frederikskirken *(see p39)*, the Marble Church **(above)** got its name on account of plans to build it with Norwegian marble. Its dome, one of the largest in Europe, has a diameter of 31 m (102 ft).

Amalienborg and Frederiksstaden

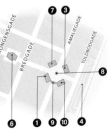

7 Christian VIII's Palace

This is where Crown Prince Frederik lived until his marriage to Australian Mary Donaldson. Part of the palace is open all year round as the Amalienborg Museum **(above)**.

8 Equestrian Statue of Frederik V

Designed and cast (1753–71) by French sculptor Jacques Saly, this bronze statue **(right)** of Frederik V is said to be more expensive than Amalienborg itself.

🔟⭐ SMK – National Gallery of Denmark

The National Gallery is housed in two buildings, one from the 19th century and the other a stylish, modern extension, linked by a bridge over Sculpture Street. The museum holds international and national paintings, sculptures, prints, drawings and installations from the 14th century to the present, with the national collection specializing in 19th-century paintings.

6 Christ as the Suffering Redeemer

This striking painting (1495–1500) on the traditional pietà theme by prominent Renaissance artist Andrea Mantegna shows the Resurrection of Christ on the third day after his crucifixion. Mantegna is known for his profound interest in ancient Roman civilization; here, it is evident in the sarcophagus upon which Christ rests.

1 The Meeting of Joachim and Anne outside the Golden Gate of Jerusalem

Filippino Lippi (1457–1504) was a true Renaissance artist. This is evident in the architectural detail of the Corinthian columns and his paintings **(above)**.

2 The Wheel of Life

Belonging to the *Suite of Seasons* series, this painting (1953) by Asger Jorn *(see p45)* represents the month of January. Jorn, who was suffering from tuberculosis, was inspired to paint this in the hope of better health.

3 The X-Room

This space has changing installations by young international artists. The black box interior is transformed into multimedia worlds.

4 Please, Keep Quiet!

Visitors have to enter this installation by Elmgreen and Dragset (2003) through swing doors, which open to a hospital ward scene. This represents the neutrality of an exhibition space.

5 Sculpture Street

An impressive, varied collection of sculptures by international contemporary artists runs the length of the building under a glass roof.

7 Alice

One of over 300 portraits by Amedeo Modigliani painted between 1915 and 1920, this beautiful painting **(below)**, with simple, stylized features, reflects the artist's interest in African sculpture.

8 Romantic Paintings

Per Kirkeby is one of Denmark's most important artists. This early collage from 1965 uses clippings from popular magazines and comics as a homage to Pop Art.

Key to Floorplan
- Ground floor
- First floor
- Second floor

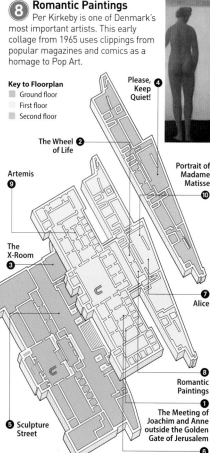

The Wheel **2** of Life

Please, **4** Keep Quiet!

Portrait of Madame Matisse **10**

Artemis **9**

The X-Room **3**

7 Alice

8 Romantic Paintings

5 Sculpture Street

1 The Meeting of Joachim and Anne outside the Golden Gate of Jerusalem

6 Christ as the Suffering Redeemer

National Gallery

9 Artemis

Created in 1893–4, Vilhelm Hammershøi's painting **(above)** shows the goddess Artemis crowned with a crescent moon. The painting's Arcadian nudity, lack of depth, muted palate and enigmatic coolness are typical of Hammershøi's later work.

10 Portrait of Madame Matisse

Also known as *The Green Stripe*, this painting by Henri Matisse of his wife was to have far-reaching repercussions in the sphere of art. It was one of many radical paintings shown in the 1905 *Salon d'Automne* and helped give rise to the Fauvist movement, known for its vibrance and spontaneous style.

NEED TO KNOW

MAP J2 ■ Sølvgade 48–50 ■ www.smk.dk

Open 10am–6pm Tue–Sun (until 8pm Wed)

Adm 120 Dkr, under-27s 95 Dkr, under-18s free

Free guided tours available

■ The children's museum provides activities and workshops every weekend throughout the summer holidays, encouraging children to make art.

■ The bright, stylish museum café looks out onto Østre Anlæg Lake. In good weather, the park is ideal for a picnic.

Museum Guide
Enter the museum from the corner of Sølvgade and Øster Voldgade. The lobby has temporary exhibitions and a bookshop. The entire ground floor is taken up by Sculpture Street, with 20th-century Danish and international art in the extension of the first and second floor. The old main building houses European art (1300–1800), Danish and Nordic art (1750–1900) as well as French art (1900–1930).

📊🔟 ⭐ Christiania

A world apart from the opulent splendour of Royal Copenhagen, this self-proclaimed "freetown" sits on the edge of one of the city's most expensive neighbourhoods. It has provided a safe haven for hippies, dreamers and nonconformists since the 1970s, when a band of ideological squatters moved into the abandoned army barracks with the aim of creating a self-sustaining community, free from the shackles of the state. Today, it's a bucolic, tumbledown wonderland of cosy cafés, bars, music venues, art galleries and shops.

Vibrant graffiti at the entrance to Christiania and Pusher Street

① Den Grå Hal
With its graffitied entrance, this is the biggest music and cultural venue in the freetown of Christiania. The former stables double up as a unique bazaar during the Christmas period, selling everything – even locally carved instruments.

② Badehuset
Dare to go bare at this back-to-basics nudist bathhouse; the cheapest and friendliest unisex sauna in the city. For under 50 Dkr, you can try a wonderful Moroccan *rasul* (a mineral cleanser).

③ Christiania Walking Tour
To really get a feel for the area, join one of the regular walking tours of Christiania and learn more about the fascinating history of the self-styled freetown from one of its residents. Tours depart regularly.

④ Nemoland
This former fruit and vegetable market is one of Copenhagen's most vibrant bars, offering cheap alcohol and food to be enjoyed on its terrace **(below)**. The outdoor stage hosts regular free concerts in summer.

5 ALIS Wonderland

What started life as a humble skate ramp has become one of the city's best skateparks. The vibrant graffiti murals **(above)** adorning the walls are now an attraction in themselves.

8 Café Månefiskeren

This cosy café with a laid-back vibe is the perfect spot to unwind or enjoy a game of bar billiards. There's regular free jazz and reggae concerts in the quaint cobblestone courtyard.

SMOKE-AWAY STALL

In 2004, as residents of Christiania sought to gain permanent rights from the government to occupy the area, they tried to appease the state by tearing down the hash stalls that brazenly lined Pusher Street at the time. One such booth, interestingly named the "Smoke-away" stall, survived intact and has been displayed in the Nationalmuseet.

10 Loppen

An intimate live music venue, Loppen **(below)** is a cornerstone of the city's alternative music scene. With gigs almost every night and a great programme that includes everything from Scandinavian punk to Danish dub-reggae, it's the ideal place to end your night out.

PRINSESSEGADE
REFSHALEVEJ
NATASJAS GADE
PUSHER ST
TINGHUSET
MALKEVEJEN

Christiania

① ⑨ ② ⑥ ⑧ ⑦ ⑩ ⑤ ④

6 Morgenstedet

Tuck into hearty vegetarian fare at this cosy cottage-style restaurant set just off Christiania's main drag. The menu changes everyday, so no two meals here are ever the same.

9 Christiania Smedie

Christiania's oldest business, this blacksmith started out producing furnaces in the early 1970s before switching its attention to building cargo bikes.

7 Galloperiet

Christiania's tongue-in-cheek tribute to the SMK – National Gallery of Denmark, this quirky gallery has a collection of wonderful arts and crafts.

NEED TO KNOW

MAP M5 ■ Prinsessegade
■ www.christiania.org

■ Christiania is a car-free community, however, you can travel there in four-wheelers and park outside. On-street parking is limited, so the easiest options are to hop on a bike or take public transport.

■ Visitors are not allowed to film or photograph in Pusher Street.

■ The possession for recreational use and sale of cannabis are still illegal in Denmark. Police officers occasionally venture into Christiania and conduct spot-checks on people leaving the commune.

🔟⭐ Slotsholmen

The small fishing village of Copenhagen was founded on the island of Slotsholmen in the 12th century. Bishop Absalon, the king's friend, built a castle here in 1167. Two centuries later, the castle was destroyed by the Hanseatic League, the European trade alliance, which resented Copenhagen's increasing control over trade. Christiansborg Slot, which stands here today, houses the Danish Parliament, the Jewish Museum and the Palace Church.

1 Christianborg Tårnet

At 106 m (348 ft), the tower of Christiansborg Slot is the highest in Copenhagen and offers a great view of the city. It is free to enter (closed Monday), but be sure to reserve in advance if you want to eat in the tower's Nordic restaurant.

2 Christiansborg Slotskirke

On the site of the original 18th-century church destroyed in the ferocious palace fire of 1794, this Neo-Classical church (see p39) was built in 1813–26. However, a fire broke out in 1992 and destroyed its roof, dome and even parts of the interior. The royal family still uses the palace chapel for baptisms as well as when royal family members lie in state.

4 Danish War Museum

Built as an arsenal in 1604–8, the Royal Danish Arsenal Museum is filled with artillery guns. The Armoury Hall has 7,000 hand weapons, some even from the 1300s.

5 Christiansborg Slot

Designed in Neo-Baroque style in 1907–28, this palace is where you will find the Folketinget (the Parliament), the Prime Ministry, the High Court and the Royal Reception Rooms (above) used for royal family functions – note the marble- and silk-adorned Throne Room and Great Hall.

3 Thorvaldsens Museum

This museum is home to almost all of the works and some of the personal belongings of Danish sculptor Bertel Thorvaldsen (see p45). In the entrance hall (below) are the original plaster casts of his most famous pieces.

6 Teatermuseet

This delightful court theatre, above the Royal Stables, was established in 1767. Now a museum (see p44), it depicts Danish theatre in the 18th and 19th centuries. Visitors can also walk onto the stage.

8 Dansk Jødisk Museum

This museum *(see p44)* has a striking, modern interior **(left)**, designed by Polish-American architect Daniel Libeskind. The building brilliantly depicts the lives and culture of the Jewish population staying in Denmark.

9 Ruins Under the Palace

These fascinating ruins were discovered during the construction of the present palace. Notable are parts of Bishop Absalon's castle, the second castle that stood here until the 18th century, and details of the routine of daily life.

CASTLE ISLAND

Several castles have stood on this island through the centuries. The first one was built in 1167 by Bishop Absalon. A second castle, used by King Erik of Pomerania, was built in 1416. When the building started to fall apart, it was pulled down and demolished in 1731 by Christian VI who, in its place, built a palace suitable for an Absolute Monarch. It was completed in 1740, but was destroyed in the fire of 1794. Another castle, built in 1803–28, burned down in 1884. The present castle was built in 1907–28.

10 Royal Library Gardens

With blossoming beds of flowers and large shadowy trees, this garden **(below)** is centered around a fountain *(see p51)*. There are plenty of benches to sit on and relax, and to admire the Galley House with its vine-strewn exterior.

7 Royal Stables

The stables of Christian VI's Palace survived the fire of 1794. The Queen's horses are still kept here amid splendid marble walls, columns and mangers. There is also a collection of royal coaches and riding gear.

NEED TO KNOW
MAP J5

Christiansborg Slotskirke: open Aug–Jun: 10am–5pm Sun; Jul: 10am–5pm daily

Thorvaldsens Museum: Bertel Thorvaldsens Plads 2; open 10am–5pm Tue–Sun; adm 80 Dkr, under-18s free; www.thorvaldsens museum.dk

Danish War Museum: 41 20 60 80; open Jan–May & Sep–Dec: 10am–5pm Tue–Sun; Jul–Aug: 10am–5pm daily

Christiansborg Slot: 33 92 64 92; open Apr–Sep: 10am–5pm daily; Oct–Mar: 10am–5pm Tue–Sun; adm 160 Dkr, students 140 Dkr, under-18s free; www.christiansborg.dk

Royal Stables: open mid-Apr–late Oct: 1:30–4pm daily; Jul & Aug: 10am–5pm daily; adm 60 Dkr, students 50 Dkr, under-18s free

Ruins Under the Palace: open Apr–Sep: 10am–5pm daily; Oct–Mar: 10am–5pm Tue–Sun; adm 60 Dkr, students 50 Dkr, under-18s free

Royal Library Gardens: 6am–10pm daily

Nationalmuseet

Denmark's largest museum, the National Museum presents the history and culture of the Danes from prehistoric times through to the present. It also houses a wonderful collection of Greek and Egyptian antiquities, an ethnographic collection and the Children's Museum. Many of the displays derive from King Frederik III's Royal Cabinet of Curiosities, put together around 1650.

NEED TO KNOW

MAP J5 ■ Ny Vestergade 10 ■ 33 13 44 11 ■ www.natmus.dk

Open Jun–Sep: 10am–6pm daily; Oct–May: 10am–5pm Tue–Sun

Adm 110 Dkr, under-18s free

Guided tours are available, check website for information

···

■ The Victorian Home, a plush apartment with beautiful, original 19th-century interiors, owned by the museum, is located nearby.

■ Have brunch or open sandwiches at one of the cafés. Restaurant Smör is fairly formal, with table service only, and serves excellent Danish cuisine.

···

Museum Guide

The entrance hall has toilets, lockers and the museum shop, selling books and educational toys with a Viking twist. The Children's Museum (see p52) is to your left. The museum's collection is spread over four floors; the ground floor has a prehistoric collection, while the first floor has a range of displays. There is a modern Danish history collection on the second floor, and the antiquities are on the third floor. Temporary exhibitions keep shifting.

1 Room 117

This 17th-century bourgeois interior can be traced to the town of Aalborg in Jutland. A room in a sea of glass-display galleries, it features a heavy wooden four-poster bed (above), chest, coffered wooden ceiling and mullioned windows.

2 Denmark's Oldest Coin

The name of Denmark and an image of a Danish king are depicted on this silver coin, displayed in Room 144, that was struck in AD 995.

5 Gundestrup Cauldron

Found near Gundestrup, this lovely silver cauldron from the Iron Age is decorated with animals and mystical figures.

3 Prehistoric Denmark and the Viking Age

One of the museum's most popular exhibits is this display of the country's 14,000-year history. These intricate golden horns (right) were reconstructed in the 20th century.

4 Cylinder Perspective Table

Part of Frederik III's Royal Cabinet of Curiosities, the table shows him and his wife painted ingeniously in a distorted perspective, rectified when viewed in the reflective cylinder.

Sun Chariot 6

The unique Sun Chariot or Solvognen **(right)** was dug up in 1902 by a farmer who was ploughing his field. This 3,400-year-old artifact from the Bronze Age shows a wheeled horse pulling a large sun disk gilded on one side.

Nationalmuseet Floorplan

Key to Floorplan
- Ground floor
- First floor
- Second floor
- Third floor

Prehistoric Denmark and the Viking Age **3**

State Rooms **8**

Room 117 **1**

Denmark's Oldest Coin **2**

Gundestrup Cauldron **5**

China, Japan and the Far East **9**

Inuit Culture **7**

Sun Chariot **6**

Oak Burial Coffins **10**

Cylinder Perspective Table **4**

China, Japan and the Far East 9

The Far East is well represented in this marvellous collection that includes Japanese laquerwork, fabulously costumed Samurai warriors, replete with weaponry, and beautiful Imperial Dragon robes.

Oak Burial Coffins 10

Seven Bronze-Age oak coffins **(below)**, dating back to 1,400 BC, occupy the ground floor. The Egtved grave, which holds the body of a fully clad young woman, is an extraordinary exhibit.

Inuit Culture 7

This collection from Greenland showcases the skill and creative ingenuity of the people of the frozen North. The displays include clothing, such as embroidered anoraks and boots, plus toys and water-colours of daily life.

State Rooms 8

The State Rooms date back to the time when this building was a royal palace. They have been well preserved and are nearly intact from the period between 1743 and 1744. Nextdoor, the Great Hall has the original Flemish tapestries.

The Top 10 of Everything

**Marble sculptures at the
Ny Carlsberg Glyptotek museum**

Moments in History

1 c 1000: Bishop Absalon's Castle

Copenhagen was founded as 'Havn' around AD 1000 on Slotsholmen (see p30) and prospered greatly from the shoals of herring that appeared in its waters. In the 1160s, Havn was given by Valdemar I to his adviser, Bishop Absalon, who built a castle as protection against raiders. The prosperity of Havn became a threat to the Hanseatic League. They attacked the castle, destroying it in 1369.

2 1443: Copenhagen, Capital of Denmark

King Erik VII (also called Erik of Pomerania) took up residence in the second castle in 1416, by which time Havn was a major economic centre. It was proclaimed the capital of Denmark in 1443.

3 1479: The Founding of the University of Copenhagen

King Christian I inaugurated the University of Copenhagen on 1 June 1479. It had four faculties – Theology, Law, Medicine and Philosophy – and

Statue of Bishop Absalon

like others of its time, was part of the Roman Catholic Church. It was re-established in 1537 by Christian III after the Reformation.

4 1534–36: Civil War and Reformation

Between 1534 and 1536, the Protestant Christian III successfully withstood an uprising against him that favoured Christian II, his Catholic cousin. The Reformation was brought to Denmark by Christian III.

5 1657: Wars with Sweden

The Swedes and Danes were in dispute over the Sound. In 1657, the Swedes crossed the Sound on foot, attacking Copenhagen. The Treaty of Roskilde saw Denmark cede its Swedish territories.

6 1660: Absolute Monarchy

Frederik III introduced Absolute Monarchy in 1660, enhancing the powers of the middle classes of Copenhagen. Later, in 1848, it was abolished by Frederik VII.

Painting of Copenhagen in 1660

7 1728: The Great Fire

In October, within four days, the greatest fire in the history of Copenhagen wiped out almost the entire north of the city. It began early in the morning at Vester Kvarter 146 – now roughly at the top of Strøget. Five churches, the university library and 1,600 houses were destroyed.

8 1801 and 1807: The Battles of Copenhagen

Early in the 19th century, the city suffered more lasting damage when the British attacked in 1801, destroying the Danish navy, and again in 1807 to discourage the Danes from supporting France in the Napoleonic Wars.

The Battles of Copenhagen

9 1943: Rescue of the Danish Jews

The Nazis occupied Denmark during World War II from 1940 to 1945. In 1943, when they ordered that all Danish Jews were to be deported to Germany, a collective of Danes and Swedes secretly evacuated virtually the entire Jewish population to Sweden by sea. As a result, most Danish Jews survived the war.

10 1999: The Øresund Bridge

Connecting Copenhagen to Malmö, Sweden, the Øresund Bridge is an impressive piece of architecture. The bridge also has significant symbolic meaning, representing a collaboration between the Swedes and the Danes, who were arch enemies in the past.

TOP 10 HISTORICAL FIGURES

A portrait of King Harald Bluetooth

1 Harald Bluetooth (911–987)
King Harald converted the country of Denmark to Christianity.

2 King Cnut (994/5–1035)
Cnut ruled England, Norway and Denmark for 20 years and famously failed to hold back the waves.

3 Bishop Absalon (1128–1201)
Counsellor to King Valdemar I, he built the first castle on Slotsholmen.

4 Tycho Brahe (1546–1601)
Brahe's astronomical tables were used to plot the rules of planetary motion.

5 Vitus Jonassen Bering (1681–1741)
A Danish navigator who lent his name to the Bering Strait, Sea, Island and Land Bridge.

6 Hans Christian Ørsted (1777–1851)
Danish physicist and chemist who discovered electromagnetism.

7 Søren Kierkegaard (1813–55)
A Danish philosopher who first put forward the theory of "existentialism".

8 Matilde Bajer (1840–1934)
Matilde founded the Danish Women's Society (one of the oldest women's rights organizations in the world).

9 Knud Rasmussen (1879–1933)
The first man to cross the Northwest Passage by dogsled.

10 Niels Bohr (1885–1962)
A Nobel Prize-winner (1922), Bohr's research contributed vastly to the understanding of quantum mechanics.

🔟 Churches

The magnificent gilded Baroque altarpiece inside Holmens Kirke

1 Holmens Kirke

Built from 1562–3 as a naval forge, it was converted into a church (see p41) in 1619. The pulpit is the tallest in Denmark, and the Baroque altarpiece is exceptionally ornate.

2 Grundtvigs Kirke

På Bjerget 14B, Bispebjerg ▪ 35 81 54 42 ▪ Open 9am–4pm Mon–Sat (until 6pm Thu), noon–4pm Sun (Nov–Apr: until 1pm) ▪ www. grundtvigskirke.dk

This parish church was built from 1921–6 by P V Jensen Klint and Kaare Klint. It has yellow-brick walls and a modern Gothic appearance.

3 Trinitatis Kirke

Standing next door to the Rundetaarn is the Trinitatis Kirke (see p19). Commissioned by Christian IV in 1637, this lovely church was completed during the reign of Frederik III in 1656. The present interior dates back to 1731, as the original was burnt in the fire of 1728. It includes boxed pews with seashell carvings, a gilded altarpiece, a Baroque dark wood pulpit and a fabulous gold and silver organ.

4 Christians Kirke

Built in the Rococo style in 1755–9 by Nicolai Eigtved, Frederik V's master architect, Christians Kirke (see p93) is starkly different from most Danish churches. Instead of the congregation sitting only in pews in the nave, the church has a second gallery level (like that of a theatre) where all the important worshippers were seated.

5 Vor Frelsers Kirke

This splendid Baroque church (see p94) was built in 1682–96 at the behest of Christian V. The king's royal insignia can be seen at various places in the church, including on the organ

The grand façade of Grundtvigs Kirke

case, which is supported by elephants, the symbol of Denmark's highly prestigious Order of the Elephant (see p43). The spire is 90 m (295 ft) high, and the tower affords a magnificent view of the city. The interior of the church is bright and well lit, thanks to the white walls and tall windows.

6 Helligåndskirken

Dating back to the 12th century, these are among the oldest architectural remains of Copenhagen. Only Helligåndshuset (now used for markets and monthly exhibitions), Christian IV's Baroque portal and Griffenfeld's Chapel survive. Much of the original church (see p19) burned down in the fire of 1728. The church re-opened after reconstruction in 1732.

7 Vor Frue Kirke

Known as Copenhagen Cathedral, the church (see p19) has been rebuilt multiple times on this site since the 12th century and has played host to royal and national events over the years. It has a 19th-century façade and a bright interior dominated by statues of Christ and his Apostles.

8 Sankt Petri Kirke

This is the city's oldest church (see pp18–19). Unlike most medieval buildings, it survived the fire of 1728. Its tower, nave and choir date back

to the 15th century, while the north and south transepts were added years later in 1634.

9 Christiansborg Slotskirke

The original 18th-century Rococo creation (see pp30–31) was destroyed in the fire of 1794 and was rebuilt in a Neo-Classical style. Inaugurated on Whit Sunday in 1826, it succumbed to another fire in 1992, but has now been rebuilt.

Ornate interior of Marmorkirken

10 Marmorkirken

This church (see pp24–5), designed in the shape of a circle by Nicolai Eigtved in 1740, has an imposing presence. Work on the building was suspended in 1770 because of increasing expenses and resumed after nearly 150 years. Eventually, it was inaugurated on 19 August 1894.

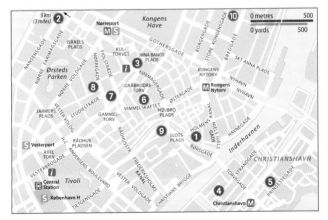

🔟 Landmark Buildings

Entrance to the Rundetaarn

1 Rundetaarn
This curious Round Tower *(see p18)* was built by Christian IV and affords a wonderful view over the city's old town. It also has a popular gallery that holds innovative, changing exhibitions.

2 Den Sorte Diamant
The Black Diamond *(see p64)* was built by architects Schmidt, Hammer and Lassen. It houses the National Museum of Photography, the Queen's Hall concert space, an exhibition area and Søren K, a smart restaurant. The shiny tiled exterior *(see p12)* is highly reflective and a popular photo opportunity for the boat-trippers floating past.

Garden at Frederiksborg Slot

3 Børsen
MAP K5 ▪ Børsgade ▪ Closed to the public
The stock exchange is remarkable for its tower with a striking spire design. The three crowns at the top of the building represent Denmark, Sweden and Norway.

4 Rosenborg Slot
This turreted Renaissance castle was built by Christian IV. Now a royal museum *(see pp16–17)*, it provides a vivid picture of the monarchy over the centuries. The crown jewels are in the basement.

5 Regensen
Built by Christian IV in the 17th century as a student hostel, Regensen *(see p18)* still houses college students. Unfortunately, most of the original building was burnt down in the city fire of 1728, but it was rebuilt shortly after.

6 Christiansborg Slot
This Neo-Baroque palace *(see pp30–31)* from the early 20th century is the seat of the government and the fifth palace to have been built on the site. Visit the ruins of the first two castles, the theatre and stables, the Royal Kitchen as well as the Royal Reception Rooms.

7 Frederiksborg Slot
This beautiful, grand Renaissance castle *(see p100)* is a short train ride out of the city. Originally built by Christian IV, it now houses The Museum of National History. Don't miss the castle's ornate chapel.

⑧ Radisson Collection Royal Hotel, Copenhagen

Designed by Danish architect Arne Jacobsen, this hotel *(see p116)* underwent a makeover in the 1980s. The original interior was retained only in Room 606; if it is unoccupied you might be able to have a look at it. The foyer has a 1960s retro look and includes Jacobsen's Swan and Egg chairs *(see p88)*. You can enjoy views of the city from the restaurant.

⑨ Operaen

The Opera House *(see pp94–5)* auditorium is a masterpiece of acoustic design, from the velour seats that don't absorb sound to the distance from the front of the stage to the back wall, which allows for the perfect time to achieve greatest clarity. Over 100,000 pieces of 23.75 carat gold leaf make up the ceiling.

Waterfront Operaen

⑩ Holmens Kirke

MAP K5 ▪ Holmens Kanal
▪ 33 13 61 78 ▪ Open 10am–4pm daily

The only Renaissance church in Copenhagen, Holmens Kirke was built as a sailors' forge in 1562–3 and converted into a church by Christian IV in 1619. The metal fence depicts the royal Danish elephant – golden elephants carrying black castles on their backs.

TOP 10 STATUES

Visit Carlsberg's Elephant Gate

1 The Elephant Gate
MAP A6
Huge statues of elephants greet visitors at the Visit Carlsberg gate.

2 Gefionspringvandet
MAP M2
Fountain depicting the goddess Gefion *(see p80)* as she drives an animal-led chariot and ploughs Zealand.

3 Fiskerkone
MAP J4
The *Fishwife* was created in 1940 and installed at this spot.

4 Lurblæserne
MAP H5
It is said that the *Hornblowers* will sound the Viking horns whenever a virgin passes by.

5 I am Queen Mary
MAP M2
This statue memorializes Denmark's colonial impact in the Caribbean and those who fought against it.

6 Zinkglobal
MAP M2
A 3-m (10-ft) figure, made from scrap materials, by Kim Michael.

7 Hans Christian Andersen
MAP H5
Famous sculpture by Henry Lukow-Nielsen *(see p72)*.

8 Hans Christian Andersen
MAP J2
Features scenes from his fairy tales.

9 Caritas Springvandet
MAP H4
One of the oldest statues in Copenhagen, dating back to 1608.

10 The Little Mermaid
MAP M1
This is the city's icon *(see p80)*, inspired by the famous fairy tale.

🔟 Sights of Royal Copenhagen

Chandeliers and tapestries in the opulent Great Hall of Christiansborg Slot

① Christiansborg Slot

This is the fifth castle *(see p30)* on this site. The first, Bishop Absalon's fortified castle (1167), was destroyed in 1369. The castle, built in 1740, was the first to be called Christiansborg and was destroyed by fire in 1794. Today, the castle houses the Danish Parliament as well as the Royal Reception Rooms.

② Fredensborg Slot

Slottet 1B, 3480 Fredensborg
■ 33 95 42 00 ■ Bus 365R, 370R
■ **Palace: open Jul–early Aug:**
12:30–4pm; gardens: open Jul:
9am–5pm daily ■ Palace: adm
■ **Guided tours available**

This Baroque palace is the summer home of the Queen. Its gardens are among the largest in Denmark.

③ Kronborg Slot

This castle *(see p104)*, built as a fortress in the 15th century, was used as a prison and army barracks until 1922. It is now occasionally used for royal functions. You may even hear a salute being fired whenever the royal yacht passes by.

④ Frederiksborg Slot

Christian IV built this Dutch Renaissance-style castle *(see p100)* between 1602 and 1620. It is notable for its spires, copper roofs and sweeping gables. After it was destroyed in a fire in 1859, the Carlsberg Brewery magnate J C Jacobsen helped to rebuild it. The castle's gardens are the only royal gardens to have escaped being updated to the 19th-century Romantic style.

⑤ Amalienborg

Two of the palaces *(see pp24–5)* here are open to the public, but the other two serve as royal homes. Queen Margrethe lives in Christian IX's Palace and Crown Prince Frederik in Frederik VIII's Palace.

**The majestic
Fredensborg Slot**

Crown Jewels
These symbols (see p16) of monarchy, kept in the stronghold basement of Rosenborg Slot, include the crown, sceptre, orb, sword of state, ampulla (flask for anointing the monarch) and royal jewellery.

 Rosenborg Slot
This delightful Renaissance palace (see pp16–17) is the oldest royal palace still standing in its original form. Set in Kongens Have, it also has a delightful rose garden.

8 Royal Copenhagen Porcelain
The traditional Royal Copenhagen design, "Blue Floral", dates back to the factory's (see p73) origins in 1775. The pottery features a blue design because in earlier times cobalt was the only colour able to withstand extremely high firing temperatures.

Pottery at Royal Copenhagen

9 Roskilde Domkirke
This city landmark is the royal burial church. Forty elaborate tombs contain both the earliest Christian monarchs and more recent ones. This 13th-century cathedral (see p102) is also a UNESCO World Heritage Site.

10 Vor Frue Kirke
Copenhagen Cathedral (see p19) has been a place of royal ceremony since the 13th century and was the setting for the marriage of Margrethe I to King Håkon VI of Norway in 1363. The weddings of Christian I (1449) and Crown Prince Frederik (2004) also took place here.

TOP 10 CROWN JEWELS

1 Christian IV's Crown
Made in 1595–6 by Dirich Fyring, this crown features diamonds, gold, enamel and pearls.

2 The Queen's Crown
The large, square, table-cut diamonds in Queen Sophie Magdalene's crown of 1731 are believed to have come from Queen Sophie Amalie's crown (1648).

3 Baptismal Set
Four-piece gold and silver baptismal set (1671), thought to have been first used for Crown Prince Frederik.

4 Regalia
Sceptre, orb, globe and ampulla made for Frederik III's coronation. Used at subsequent coronations until 1840.

5 Order of the Elephant
The order was founded by Christian I around 1460. The chain is made of gold, enamel, diamonds and pearls.

6 Order of the Dannebrog
Established in 1671 as part of the measures introduced by the Absolute monarchs to manage their subjects.

7 Jewellery Sets
Includes a pearl set (1840) made from Charlotte Amalie's jewellery, a diamond set and an emerald set (18th century).

8 Oldenburg Horn
This is an enamelled, silver-gilt drinking horn.

9 The King's Law 1665
Absolutism's constitution, made from parchment, silk, gold and silver.

10 Christian V's Crown
Christian V's Absolutist crown (1670–71) has a large, rare sapphire believed to be a present from the Duke of Milan to Christian I in 1474.

The stunning crown of Christian V

Museums and Galleries

The Danish Jødisk Museum

1 Dansk Jødisk Museum

MAP K5 ■ Proviantpassangen 6 ■ 33 11 22 18 ■ Opening hours vary, check website ■ Adm, free with Copenhagen City Pass, under-18s free ■ www.jewmus.dk

The Danish Jewish Museum tells the story of Denmark's Jewish community. Designed by architect Daniel Libeskind, the interlocking interior symbolizes good Danish–Jewish relations, its apogee being the rescue of 7,000 Jews from the Nazis.

2 Designmuseum Danmark

Denmark's largest museum (see p79) devoted to design, the Designmuseum holds cutting-edge Danish 20th- and 21st-century designs. Exhibits are varied and include furniture, textiles, silver-ware and more. It also hosts special international exhibitions. Visitors can participate in a variety of activities organized for families.

3 Teatermuseet

MAP J5 ■ Christiansborg Ridebane 18 ■ 33 11 51 76 ■ Opening times vary, check website ■ Adm ■ www.teatermuseet.dk

On display at this museum are sections including the stage, the auditorium and dressing rooms of the 18th-century Royal Theatre (see p46) that survived the devastating fire of 1794.

4 Frihedsmuseet

The Museum of Danish Resistance (see p79) explores Danish life during the Nazi occupation of 1940–45. Several poignant installations document its effect on the general population and its role in spurring the resistance movement.

5 Nationalmuseet

At Denmark's largest museum of cultural history (see pp32–3) explore the history of the Danes up to the present day. Artifacts range from Iron Age burials and Renaissance interiors to African masks and houses on stilts. Check out the museum's ethnographic collection, including several rooms devoted to the Inuit.

6 Ny Carlsberg Glyptotek

This museum (see p70) houses a fabulous collection of antiquities from the Mediterranean coast, Egypt, Greece and Rome. You will also find an impressive collection of 19th- and 20th-century Danish and French fine art on display.

The Ny Carlsberg Glyptotek

7 Cisternerne – The Cisterns

Beneath the manicured lawns of Frederiksberg Have, this exhibition space *(see p88)* is remarkable for both its provocative contemporary art and film installations as well as the singularity of its setting, a 19th-century cistern.

8 Davids Samling

Set inside a 19th-century townhouse, the museum *(see p78)* holds the collections of Christian Ludvig David (1878–1960), a Danish barrister. It includes some fabulous furniture as well as ancient Islamic ornamental art.

The grand façade of SMK

9 SMK – National Gallery of Denmark

Nestled in a park with lakes and grassy slopes, the SMK *(see pp26–7)* displays a collection of international art, with works by Great Masters like Dürer and Titian and by icons such as Picasso and Matisse. These are displayed with 20th-century Danish works, including those of the CoBrA group.

10 Thorvaldsens Museum

Opened in 1848, this museum *(see pp30–31)* pays homage to the Neo-Classical sculptor Bertel Thorvaldsen. It includes most of his works, as well as some private belongings. You can also visit his grave.

TOP 10 DANISH ARTISTS

Sculpture by Bertel Thorvaldsen

1 Bertel Thorvaldsen (1770–1844)
Son of an Icelandic wood carver, Thorvaldsen became Denmark's most famous sculptor.

2 Christoffer Eckersberg (1783–1853)
Laid the foundations for Denmark's zenith of painting (1800–50).

3 Michael Ancher (1849–1927)
One of the best-known artists in Denmark and the unofficial head of the Skagen group.

4 Peder Severin Krøyer (1851–1909)
His work is inspired by the lives of the fishermen of Skagen.

5 Anna Ancher (1859–1935)
A Skagen artist and wife of Michael Ancher. Her work is typified by picturesque scenes of family life.

6 Vilhelm Hammershøi (1864–1916)
Known for his paintings of interiors, done in muted colours.

7 Richard Mortensen (1910–1993)
The first Danish artist to turn to abstraction. Also known for his perfect technical finish.

8 Asger Jorn (1914–73)
Founder of CoBrA, an important art group to emerge after World War II.

9 Bjørn Nørgaard (b 1947)
One of the most influential Danish contemporary artists, his works span a range of fields, including sculpture. He also designed the Queen's Tapestries.

10 Olafur Eliasson (b 1967)
Danish-Icelandic artist who erects fascinating kinetic sculptures inspired by natural phenomena in cities around the world.

🔟 Hans Christian Andersen Sights

Hotel d'Angleterre, overlooking gardens

① Hotel d'Angleterre

Hans Christian Andersen lived in Hotel d'Angleterre (see p114) in November 1860, when he occupied two rooms at the corner of Kongens Nytorv and Østergade (Strøget), close to the Royal Theatre. He also stayed here between August 1869 and March 1870, and, finally, during April and May 1871.

② Det Kongelige Teater

Andersen arrived in the city on 6 September 1819 as a starstruck 14-year-old boy. It was "my second birthday", he recounts in his 1855 biography, The Fairy Tale of My Life. Determined to become an actor, he went straight to the Royal Theatre (see p23) in search of a job. Although he was occasionally employed as an actor, his acting talent never quite matched his skill as a writer.

③ Lille Kongensgade 1
MAP K4

On 23 October 1866, Andersen took a suite of rooms on the third floor of Lille Kongensgade 1, rented to him by a photographer, Thora Hallager. It was here that he bought furniture for the first time in his life (at the age of 61), as the apartment was an unfurnished one.

④ Rundetaarn

The exhibition space (see pp18–19) here was once the university library where Andersen spent many hours. His fairy tale, The Tinderbox (1835), talks of a dog with "two eyes, each of which is as big as the Round Tower" guarding a treasure. This is quite fitting, since Rundetaarn was originally built as an observatory.

⑤ Vingårdsstræde 6
MAP K4

Andersen lived here (then No 132) for a year in 1827 in a spartan garret room, preparing for his university exams. This is where he wrote the poem The Student. Once a museum, the room is no longer open to visitors.

⑥ Bakkehuset

The Bakkehuset (House on the Hill) was the home of prominent literary patron Knud Lyne Rahbek and his wife, Kamma, from 1802 to 1830. Andersen met the couple in the early 1820s and their home (see p89) soon became a meeting place for poets and authors.

The elegant interior of Bakkehuset

7 Nyhavn Nos 18, 20 and 67

Andersen lived in lodgings on and around Nyhavn (see p22) for much of his life, including at Nyhavn 280 (now No 20) in 1834, No 67 in 1848 and No 18 (a private hotel) in 1871. He lived here until 1875, when he fell terminally ill and moved in with the Melchiors, who then nursed him in their own home.

8 Assistens Kirkegård

This is the cemetery (see p77) where Andersen's body was interred in Nørrebro. The stone is inscribed with inspirational lines from his poem *Oldingen*, also known as *The Old Man* (1874).

Hans Christian Andersen's grave

9 Magasin du Nord

In 1838, Andersen moved into Hotel du Nord, now the department store Magasin du Nord (see pp22–3). Here he proceeded to rent two rooms in the attic, one of which overlooked the Royal Theatre. The next-door Mini's Café became a regular haunt for the writer.

10 Vor Frue Kirke

Andersen died on 4 August 1875 of liver cancer. His funeral, a national event attended by the king and crown prince, was held at Vor Frue Kirke (see p19) in the old town.

🔟 Outdoor Activities

Browsing the flea market at Nørrebro

1 Flea Markets

Frederiksberg Rådhusplads:
MAP A5; open Apr–Oct: 9am–3pm
Sat ■ Bertel Thorvaldsens Plads:
MAP J5; open May–Sep: 8am–5pm
Fri ■ Ravnsborggade, Nørrebro:
MAP D3; open Mar–Nov: 10am–
4pm Sun

There are many outdoor flea
markets in the summer, offering
everything from furniture to vinyl.

2 CopenHot

Refshalevej 325 ■ 31 32
78 08 ■ www.copenhot.com
The purveyors of Copenhagen's
only floating hot-tub experience,
this open-air spa brings Nordic
wellness to the city centre. With
three giant hot tubs, a sauna with
panoramic views of the harbour
and five "sailing spa" boats, it's the
perfect place to escape the hustle
and bustle of the city. There's even
speakers to play your own music.

3 Bikes

Almost every major road
in Copenhagen has a cycle lane
and you can hire a bike (see p109).

4 GoBoat

Islands Brygge 10
■ 40 26 10 25 ■ en.goboat.dk
If you prefer to explore the city's
waterways at your own pace, hop
on board a solar-powered GoBoat
and spend an afternoon chugging
through the canals. You can buy
a picnic hamper or champagne to
take on board, although the captain
must always remain sober while
in control of their vessel.

5 Lounging by the Lakes

Artificial lakes divide the
main city from Nørrebro and
Østerbro. Of these, Skt Jørgens Sø,
Peblinge Sø and Sortedams Sø are
easily accessible. You can lounge
along their grassy banks or enjoy
the scenic view from the bridges.

6 Kongens Have

Attached to Rosenborg Slot,
the King's Garden (see p17) is a
great place to sunbathe, play fris-
bee, cricket or football, or have a
picnic. In the summer, you can catch
a puppet show or a jazz concert.

7 Canal tours

Harbour and canal tours are a
good way to see the city. There are two
canal tour companies (see pp12–13).

Canal tour in Nyhavn

8 Assistens Kirkegård

Take a walk through this meandering churchyard *(see p77)*, which holds the graves of famous Danes like Hans Christian Andersen, August Bournonville and Niels Bohr.

9 Dyrehaven

MAP B2 ■ Dyrehaven, Klampenborg

A short trip north from Copenhagen, this deer park is a UNESCO World Heritage Site. It has been here since the 16th century and is home to over 2,000 deer. It has lush forests, small lakes, wide landscapes and a theme park, Bakken *(see p52)*.

Frederiksberg Have's garden

10 Frederiksberg Have

Set against the backdrop of Frederiksberg Slot, this is a stunning garden *(see p87)*. Explore its lawns and canals and you might even be rewarded with a glimpse of the elephants at Zoologisk Have *(see p88)*.

TOP 10 BEACHES AND POOLS

Diving at Havnebadet

1 Havnebadet
Floating harbour pool *(see p64)* with fresh water.

2 Bellevue
MAP B2 ■ Strandvejen 340, 2930 Klampenborg
Full of people playing, sailing or relaxing. The left end is nudist.

3 Fælledparkens Soppesø
MAP D2 ■ Borgmester Jensens Allé 50, Østerbro
Huge, child-friendly, outdoor pool.

4 Amager Strandpark
MAP B3 ■ Amager Strandvej
Luxury Beach with lagoon, artificial island and snack kiosks.

5 Køge Bugt Strandpark
MAP B3 ■ Ishøj Store Torv 20, 2635 Ishøj
A 7-km (4-mile) beach along Køge Bay.

6 Bellahøj Svømmestadion
MAP B3 ■ Bellahøjvej 1–3, Brønshøj
Indoor and outdoor swimming facilities, including water slides.

7 Frederiksdal Friluftsbad
MAP B2 ■ Frederiksdal Badesti 1, Virum ■ 45 83 81 85
Gorgeous lakeside beach with café.

8 DGI-Byen
MAP D5 ■ Corner of Tietgensgade & Ingerslevsgade ■ 33 29 80 00
Indoor sports hall and a swimming pool.

9 Charlottenlund Beach
MAP B2 ■ Park Strandvejen 144, Charlottenlund
Good place for sunbathing.

10 Copencabana Havnebadet ved Fisketorvet
MAP E6 ■ Kalvebod Brygge 55, Vesterbro ■ 35 42 68 60
A floating harbour pool.

🔟 Off the Beaten Track

The bustling Sydhavnen harbour

1 Sydhavnen Harbour
MAP D6 ■ Nordre Toldbod 7, 1259 København

The waterfront area of Sydhavnen may be glassy and modern, but stray into its older parts and a more rustic scene awaits. The small fishing boats moored in this miniature time capsule only add to the charm. Check out Café Syd for a local meal – for which you'll need to pay with cash, as that's all they accept here.

2 GoMonkey
MAP B2 ■ Vandtårnsvej 55, Søborg ■ 25 53 30 22 ■ Open 9am–7pm daily

Channel your inner Tarzan at this suburban climbing park in Søborg, which is a 15-minute train ride from central Copenhagen. There are zip-lines, rope bridges, high-wires and swing ropes.

3 Meyers Madhus
MAP C3 ■ Nørrebrogade 52 C ■ 35 36 38 37 ■ Open 10am–3pm Mon–Fri

If you'd like to learn how to cook New Nordic, get schooled by the master himself at one of celebrity chef and restaurateur Claus Meyer's Nørrebro cookery classes. Large groups are welcome, but early booking is advised.

4 Amager Strand Beach Park
MAP C3 ■ Amager Strand Promenaden 1

Featuring 4.6 km (2.9 miles) of beaches, a world-class skatepark and an open-air concert venue, this sprawling public beach park springs into life in May or June when sun-starved city-dwellers flock to the coast at the first sign of summer.

5 Dragør Havn
MAP C3 ■ Dragør, south of Copenhagen Airport

It may be less than 12 km (7 miles) from central Copenhagen, but this fishing village and marina is far away from the hustle and bustle of the city centre. This 12th-century settlement still has immaculately preserved medieval buildings in the traditional Danish style. In the evening, head down to the marina for excellent seafood at local restaurants.

Boats docked at Dragør marina

6 Noma
Refshalevej 96 ■ 32 96 32 97 ■ Open 5–11pm Wed–Sat ■ www.noma.dk

An old mining depot situated on Refshaleøen has been beautifully preserved and serves as a home for Noma, the world-famous restaurant (see p97). Credited with redefining the New Nordic culinary movement, the restaurant's dishes are based on seasonal and regional ingredients, innovative cooking techniques and beautiful plating.

7 Nordic Noir Tours
MAP D5 ■ Vesterport Station ■ www.nordicnoirtours.com

Discover the darker side of the city with a guided tour of the film locations used in hit crime dramas *Forbrydelsen* (*The Killing*), *Borgen* and *The Bridge*. Take a peek behind the scenes at each series, and venture into some of the city's lesser-known spots. Tours start from Vesterport Station, and discounts are often offered on pre-bookings.

8 Escape Copenhagen
MAP G4 ■ Nørre Farimagsgade 7 ■ 42 90 91 91 ■ www.escape-cph.dk

Put your sleuthing skills to the test at Copenhagen's premier live escape game, where you must find the hidden objects, figure out the clues and solve the puzzles to earn your freedom and escape from one of the many themed rooms.

9 Royal Library Gardens
MAP K5 ■ Proviantpassagen 1 ■ Open 6am–10pm daily

Tucked away behind Christiansborg Palace on Slotsholmen island, this secluded public park was built in 1920 on the site of King Christian IV's former naval port. The fountain in the central pool cascades every hour in a nod to the garden's fascinating maritime heritage.

Sunbathing at Royal Library Gardens

10 Sydhavns Tippen
MAP B3

Only a 20-minute bike ride away from the city centre lies this stunning Nordic savannah, replete with thorny trees, stunted shrubs, a flock of sheep and a couple of alpacas. Take a moment to admire the small, dilapidated houses lining the canal that flows towards and past ValbyParken (Musikbyen).

TOP10 Children's Attractions

Line 8 trolley bus at Tivoli, one of the family-oriented rides

1 Tivoli
The best time to take kids to Tivoli *(see pp14–15)* is during the day, when the atmosphere is more suitable for families. The park's many fun rides include cars on tracks, dragon boats on the lake, the pantomime theatre and the trolley bus.

2 Guinness World Records Museum
This highly popular attraction *(see p72)* brings the Guinness World Records to life. From the utterly bizarre, such as bicycle-eating men, to the internationally renowned in sport and science, 13 galleries celebrate numerous examples of strangeness, ingenuity and determination.

3 World of H C Andersen Museum
Explore the life of Hans Christian Andersen at this charming museum *(see p72)*. It is aimed at kids, who will enjoy the tableaux and recordings of some of his fairy tales. The manuscript of *The Stone and the Wise Man* (1858) may interest bibliophiles.

4 Nationalmuseet
Copenhagen's National Museum *(see pp32–3)* includes an interesting Children's Museum where children can explore and play with anything. They can go on a raid in the Viking ship, make food in the medieval kitchen or can armour and protect the castle against an enemy attack or even "camp out" in a Bedouin tent.

5 Bakken
MAP B2 ■ Dyrehavevej 62 ■ 39 63 35 44 ■ www.bakken.dk
If you go down to the woods, you'll find the world's oldest amusement park. Established in 1583, Bakken is a real one-off: a quirky mix of modern thrill rides and vintage sideshows that offers free entry all year round.

Kids enjoying at the Guinness Museum

6 Experimentarium

MAP B2 ▪ Tuborg Havnevej,
Hellerup ▪ 39 27 33 33 ▪ Open 9am–
5pm Mon–Sun ▪ Adm, under-2s free
▪ www.experimentarium.dk

This innovative science centre
brings science to life through play
and hands-on exploration. Most
exhibits are interactive, allowing
kids to learn through experiments,
and adults can have just as much
fun too. Children aged from 1 to 5
will find the Miniverse exciting.

7 SMK – National Gallery of Denmark

The Children's Art Museum at the
SMK (see pp26–7) caters to children
aged between 4 and 12, with workshops where kids can draw, paint
and sculpt; the museum also has a
sketching room. On the first Sunday
of each month, the museum holds
a family day, which includes guided
museum tours.

8 Dino's Legeland

MAP B3

A dinosaur-themed fantasy world
for children of all ages teeming
with colourful indoor playgrounds,
rubber slides and countless kaleidoscopic ball pits. You're welcome
to bring your own food, or sample
the affordable, specially prepared
children's menu on offer.

9 Den Blå Planet, National Aquarium Denmark

Denmark's national aquarium (see
p100) is the largest and most modern
in Northern Europe. It is home to
over 400 species of marine life. You
can catch glimpses of hammerhead
sharks, elegant rays and more.

Skaters at Fælledparken

10 Fælledparken

Copenhagen's largest public
park (see p80), in Østerbro next to the
Danish National Stadium, has a fan-
tastic playground featuring multiple
tiny trampolines and castles. There
is also a skatepark, cafés, sports
fields and numerous green lawns for
other activities. The park was created
between 1906 and 1914 by landscape
architect Edvard Glæsel.

🔟 Performing Arts and Music Venues

Tables at Wallmans Cirkusbygningen

1 Wallmans Cirkusbygningen

MAP G5 ▪ Jernbanegade 8 ▪ 33 16 37 00 ▪ www.wallmans.dk

Built between 1885 and 1886, this venue was previously a circus building. Today it is used as a glamorous setting for old-fashioned "dinner, show and dancing" evenings. The spectacular entertainment surrounds guests across seven stages while resting members of the cast serve dinner. After the show, it turns into a club.

2 Det Kongelige Teater

World-class performances of ballet are held in Kongens Nytorv (see p23), while dramatic works are performed at the playhouse on the waterfront, Skuespilhuset.

Performance at Det Kongelige Teater

3 Operaen

Famed for its acoustics, the Opera House (see pp94–5) attracts a variety of international productions. You can enjoy a good view of the stage from any seat and all the tickets are relatively cheap due to government subsidy.

4 Tivoli Concert Hall

The Tivoli Concert Hall (see pp14–15), with a capacity of 1,900, is one of the largest music venues in Copenhagen. It stages more than 100 operas, ballets and rock and jazz concerts during the Tivoli season.

5 Alice

MAP J4 ▪ Nørre Allé 7 ▪ 31 54 58 75 ▪ www.alicecph.com

One of Copenhagen's most experimental music venues, Alice offers a unique, varied programme. On weekends, late-night concerts kick off at 11pm.

6 Mojo Bluesbar

MAP H5 ▪ Løngangstræde 21C ▪ 33 11 64 53 ▪ www.mojo.dk

Atmospheric and intimate, this bar hosts blues and live jazz performances daily throughout the year.

7 Det Ny Teater
MAP C5 ▪ Gammel Kongevej 29 ▪ 33 25 50 75 ▪ www.detny teater.dk

This early 20th-century theatre hosts a variety of popular international musicals, such as *Phantom of the Opera* and *Les Misérables*.

8 Koncerthuset
MAP B3 ▪ Ørestads Boulevard 13 ▪ 35 20 62 62 ▪ www.dr.dk/ koncerthuset

The concert house of the national broadcaster Danmarks Radio (DR) was designed by Jean Nouvel. This landmark building with its blue glass fiber façade has superior acoustics.

Koncerthuset's curved interior

9 Parken
MAP D2 ▪ Per Henrik Lings Allé 2 ▪ 35 43 31 31 ▪ www.teliaparken.dk

This football stadium held its first concert in 2001 with the Eurovision Song Contest. Bands including U2 and Metallica have since performed.

10 VEGA
MAP B6 ▪ Enghavevej 40 ▪ 33 25 70 11 ▪ Opening hours vary; club nights: 11pm–4am Fri & Sat ▪ Adm ▪ www.vega.dk

Occupying a 1950s trade union building, VEGA offers club nights that attract international acts and DJs.

TOP 10 JAZZ VENUES AND EVENTS

Copenhagen Jazz Festival

1 Copenhagen Jazz Festival/ Winter Jazz
In February and July Copenhagen hosts Scandinavia's biggest jazz festival.

2 Charlie Scott's
MAP H4 ▪ Skindergade 43 ▪ 33 12 12 20
A tiny city-centre bar for jazz lovers.

3 Jazzhus Montmartre
MAP K3 ▪ Store Renegade 19a ▪ 31 72 34 94
This legendary venue seats 70 people.

4 La Fontaine
MAP J5 ▪ Kompagnistræde 11 ▪ 33 11 60 98
Known for late sessions on Fridays and Saturdays.

5 Huset-KBH
MAP J5 ▪ Rådhusstræde 13 ▪ 21 51 21 51
Culture house hosts a jazz club.

6 Jazzcup
MAP J3 ▪ Gothersgade 107 ▪ 33 33 87 40
Both a record store and a café hosting jazz sessions on weekends.

7 Sofie Kælderen
MAP L6 ▪ Overgaden Oven Vandet 32 ▪ 32 57 77 01
A cornerstone of the city's jazz scene.

8 Tango y Vinos
MAP L4 ▪ Herluf Trolles Gade 9 ▪ 22 93 98 00
Tiny Argentinian wine bar hosting jazz, flamenco, funk and tango musicians.

9 Kind of Blue
MAP D3 ▪ Ravnsborggade 17 ▪ 26 35 10 56
A small, cosy bar on a hip street.

10 Palæ Bar
MAP K4 ▪ Ny Adelgade 5 ▪ 33 12 54 71
A favourite hangout for musicians.

TOP10 Nightlife Venues

Plush, subterranean interior of Copenhagen speakeasy, The Jane

1 The Jane
MAP J4 ■ Gråbrødretorv 8 ■ 53 66 37 13 ■ Open 8pm–5am Fri–Sat ■ www.thejane.dk

A night at this part wood-panelled speakeasy, part industrial nightclub *(see p74)* is whatever you want it to be. Chat over classic cocktails and soft jazz in the library bar, or cut loose on the hidden dance floor, neatly accessed via a false bookcase.

2 Hive
MAP H4 ■ Skindergade 45–7 ■ 31 73 73 07 ■ Open 11pm–4am Fri & Sat ■ www.hivecph.dk

The city's old courthouse is now a modern nightclub with 3D wall visuals and lounge areas.

3 Rust
Trendy Rust *(see p82)* is at the cutting edge of the local music and clubbing scene. It showcases up-and-coming acts, live music sets and top international DJs.

4 Brass Monkey
MAP B6 ■ Enghavevej 31 ■ Open 8pm–1am Thu, 8pm–4am Fri & Sat ■ www.brassmonkey.dk

Swap the stresses of city life for the finest of rums at Copenhagen's Tiki bar, a kitsch wonderland of cocktails, grass skirts and hula dancers.

5 Jolene
MAP D6 ■ Flæsketorvet 81–85 ■ Open 8pm–5am Thu–Sat

Jolene's tiled backdrop is a throwback to its past as a slaughterhouse in the meatpacking district. Now a lively bar, its dance floor comes alive with classic disco and deep house favourites.

6 Bakken
MAP C6 ■ Flæsketorvet 19–21 ■ Open 10pm–5am Thu, 8pm–5am Fri & Sat ■ www.bakkenkbh.dk

Not to be confused with the family theme park in Dyrehaven *(see p49)*, this dark, dingy and achingly hip club is a favourite among young locals.

Revellers at Bakken

7 Ideal Bar

MAP B6 ▪ Enghavevej 40
▪ 33 25 70 11 ▪ Open 7pm–4am
Wed (until 5am Thu–Sat) ▪ www.
vega.dk

On the ground floor of trendy venue
VEGA *(see p55)*, this lounge bar offers
club nights with a local vibe. It is an
inexpensive midweek option.

8 Culture Box

MAP K2 ▪ Kronprinsessegade
54 ▪ 33 32 50 50 ▪ Open 11pm–6am
Fri & Sat (Culture Box Bar: open from
6pm) ▪ www.culture-box.com

This purist techno club is one of
Copenhagen's leading venues for
electronic music. Its cocktail bar
opens earlier than the club and
makes a good meeting place. For
above-18s only.

DJ at work, Culture Box

9 Mesteren og Lærlingen

MAP D6 ▪ Flæsketorvet 86
▪ Open 4pm–1am Mon (until 2am Tue
& Wed, 3am Thu, 3:30am Fri & Sat)

One of the oldest and cosiest
drinking holes in the meatpacking
district, Mesteren og Lærlingen
offers draft beer, delectable food
and some of the best soul, hip
hop and disco nights in town.

10 Chateau Motel

MAP D5 ▪ Knabrostraede 3
▪ 53 89 31 34 ▪ Open 11pm–5am
Fri & Sat

Whether you want to dance or sip
your cocktails quietly, Chateau Motel
(see p92) is the place to be at. Each
floor here has its own music profile.

TOP 10 MICROBREWERIES

The beer menu at Warpigs

1 Warpigs
MAP C6 ▪ Flæsketorvet 25 ▪ 43
48 48 48 ▪ www.warpigs.dk
Brewed on site, with 20 taps daily.

2 Nørrebro Bryghus
MAP D3 ▪ Ryesgade 3, Nørrebro ▪ 35
30 05 30 ▪ www.noerrebrobryghus.dk
Tour this brewery and taste some beer.

3 Fermentoren Beer Bar
MAP C6 ▪ Halmtorvet 29C
▪ 23 90 86 77
House brand brewed by Dry & Bitter
with a selection of other craft beers.

4 BRUS
MAP C3 ▪ Guldbergsgade 29 ▪ 75
22 22 00 ▪ www.tapperietbrus.dk
With 32 beers on tap and an on-site
restaurant, this slick brewpub has it all.

5 Brewpub
MAP H5 ▪ Vestergade 29 ▪ 33 32 00
60 ▪ Closed Sun ▪ www.brewpub.dk
Includes a 17th-century beer garden.

6 Bryggeriet Apollo
MAP G5 ▪ Vesterbrogade 3
▪ 33 12 33 13 ▪ www.bryggeriet.dk
The original local microbrewery.

7 Ølsnedkeren
MAP C4 ▪ Griffenfeldsgade 52
▪ www.olsnedkeren.dk
This brewery has 12 rotating taps.

8 Amager Bryghus
MAP C5 ▪ Kirstinehøj 38B ▪ 32 50
62 00 ▪ www.amagerbryghus.dk
Tours Mon–Sat by appointment.

9 Mikkeller
Viktoriagade 8, Vesterbro
▪ 33 31 04 15 ▪ www.mikkeller.dk
A famous craft beer pub in Denmark.

10 Kølsters Tolv Haner
MAP C3 ▪ Rantzausgade 56
▪ 32 20 94 84
This place serves its own ever-changing
selection of ecological beer and cider.

LGBTQ+ Venues

1 Centralhjørnet
MAP H4 ▪ Kattesundet 18
▪ 33 11 85 49 ▪ Open noon–2am daily (until 4am Fri & Sat) ▪ www.centralhjornet.dk

This is Copenhagen's oldest gay bar, dating from 1852. It hosts drag nights, but regular shows take place every Thursday. Kylie Minogue and Europop are jukebox favourites here and Sunday afternoons are usually packed with people dancing.

2 Jailhouse CPH
MAP H4 ▪ Studiestræde 12
▪ 33 15 22 55 ▪ Open 2pm–2am Sun–Thu (until 5am Fri & Sat); restaurant: 6–9pm Thu & Fri ▪ www.jailhousecph.dk

Kitted out as a prison, this café and event bar has a relaxed atmosphere. The booths are designed like prison cells and staff is dressed as prison guards or police officers. There is a restaurant on the second floor.

3 Oscar Bar and Café
MAP H5 ▪ Regnbuepladsen 7
▪ 33 12 09 99 ▪ Open 11am–11pm Sun–Thu, 11am–2am Fri & Sat (kitchen: 11am–4pm & 5–9:30pm daily) ▪ www.oscarbarcafe.dk

An evening bar and café with a long bar and posh leather furniture. The DJ plays funky disco and soulful deep house during the weekends.

Seating at Oscar Bar and Café

Drinks at Masken Bar & Café

4 Masken Bar & Café
MAP H4 ▪ Studiestræde 33
▪ 33 91 09 37 ▪ Open 2pm–3am Sun–Thu (until 5am Fri & Sat)
▪ www.maskenbar.dk

One of the oldest LGBTQ+ bars, Masken hosts live music and drag shows.

5 Café Intime
MAP B5 ▪ Allégade 25, 2000 Frederiksberg ▪ 38 34 19 58 ▪ Open 4pm–2am daily ▪ www.cafeintime.dk

Founded in 1913, this kitsch bar has a predominantly gay crowd. A pianist plays popular classics; you can also enjoy jazz on Sundays.

6 G-A-Y Copenhagen
MAP H4 ▪ Vester Voldgade 10
▪ 33 14 13 30 ▪ Open 4pm–3am Thu (until 5am Fri & Sat)

A highly recommended gay night club with drag shows. Music here focuses on pop hits and mainstream tracks.

7 Mens Bar
MAP H4 ■ Teglgårdsstræde 3
■ 33 12 73 03 ■ Open 4pm–2am daily
■ www.mensbar.dk

This strictly all-male, no-frills bar is filled with leather, fascinating tattoos and a dash of denim. Try to catch the free Danish brunch at 3pm available on the first Sunday of every month.

8 Never Mind Bar
MAP G4 ■ Nørre Voldgade
■ Open 10pm–6am daily ■ www.nevermindbar.dk

The party rarely stops at this popular, central nightclub. It's an accessible-for-all space – come as you are and have a blast into the wee hours of the morning. You are welcome to request your own song.

9 Cosy Bar
MAP H4 ■ Studiestræde 24
■ 33 12 74 27 ■ Open 8pm–5am Fri & Sat ■ www.cosybar.dk

One of Copenhagen's oldest gay bars, Cosy has a small dancefloor. It is often packed with a young crowd and is best visited after 1am.

10 Vela
MAP C5 ■ Viktoriagade 2–4 ■ 26 30 23 18 ■ Open 9pm–2am Thu, 9pm–5am Fri & Sat ■ www.velagayclub.dk

Attracting a mixed crowd, Vela is a popular lesbian bar in the Vesterbro area of Copenhagen. Expect cheap beer, table football and cosy booths.

TOP 10 LGBTQ+ FESTIVALS AND EVENTS

Copenhagen Pride Festival

1 Danish Rainbow Awards
Apr
This annual LGBTQ+ award show is organized by the Copenhagen Gay & Lesbian Chamber of Commerce.

2 Distortion
End May–Jun
An inclusive five-day techno music festival that takes place during the day on the streets of Copenhagen.

3 St Hans
23 Jun
This is an annual bonfire and beach party held on Amager Beach on Sankt Hans Night.

4 Malmö Pride Festival
Jun ■ www.malmopride.com
Across the bridge, this jamboree was previously called the Rainbow Festival.

5 Copenhagen Pride Festival
Aug ■ www.copenhagenpride.dk
This is a week-long festival where festivities include the gay pride parade.

6 Mix Copenhagen Film Festival
Oct ■ www.mixcopenhagen.dk
Held over ten days, this is one of Denmark's oldest LGBTQ+ film festivals.

7 World Aids Day
1 Dec
Commemorated each year.

8 Nordic Open
30 Dec ■ www.pandans.dk/nordic
A popular dance contest for same-sex couples held each year.

9 GAY CPH App
For more events while exploring the city, download this free app.

10 Pan Idræt
www.panidraet.dk
This LGBTQ+ multi-sports club is home to the popular field hockey team, the Copenhagen Black Swans.

🔟 Restaurants

Asian-inspired furniture and tropical flowers at Kiin Kiin

① Selma

MAP D4 ■ Rømersgade 20
■ 40 27 72 03 ■ Open 11:30am–
4pm Wed–Mon, 6:30–11pm Thu–Sat
■ www.selmacopenhagen.dk ■ ⓚⓚ

This restaurant serves the city's best *smørrebrød*, which departs from traditional flavours and veers toward experimental and alternative presentations. While mentioned in Michelin guides, Selma maintains an affordable menu that changes with the seasons.

② Aamann's 1921

Copenhagen's *smørrebrød* king serves arguably the best sandwiches in town, and reinvents Danish dishes. From fried chicken with lingonberries to shrimp on toast made from house-ground flour, this kitchen *(see p75)* is rewardingly obsessed with detail.

③ Kona

MAP B6 ■ Bag
Elefanterne 15 ■ Closed
Sun & Mon ■ www.
behind-the-elephants.
com ■ ⓚⓚⓚ

Come here for "Izakaya", a snack-based menu in a relaxed setting, or "Omakase", a seasonal eight-course menu consisting of locally sourced seafood.

④ Kiin Kiin

Dining at Europe's only Michelin-starred Thai restaurant *(see p83)* is a feast for the senses. Start by sipping Champagne and scoffing street food in the underground snug, and then follow your nose upstairs to the lemongrass and bamboo-scented dining room for a master-class in modern Thai cooking.

⑤ Alchemist

MAP B2 ■ Refshalevej 173C
■ 31 71 61 61 ■ Open 5pm–2am
Wed–Sat ■ www.alchemist.dk
■ ⓚⓚⓚ

Set in an industrial neighbourhood on the island of Refshaleøen, the Alchemist offers expertly curated dishes that are technically complex, highly creative and enhanced by art, drama, music, sensory stimulation and visual technology.

⑥ Formel B

Beautifully prepared, French-style cuisine using fresh Danish ingredients is the key to the dishes served in this charming restaurant *(see p91)*, which prides itself on supporting animal welfare and sustainability. Sample raw marinated shrimps with squid and soy-ginger browned butter.

Beautifully plated dish at Formel B

⑦ Noma

Ranked the world's best restaurant five times, Noma *(see p97)* has helped put New Nordic cuisine on the world map. The experimental tasty menu is divided into three seasonal themes: seafood, vegetables, and game and forest. Be sure to make a booking before the restaurant closes in 2024.

⑧ Geranium

MAP D2 ▪ Per Henrik Lings Alle 4 ▪ Open 6–11pm Wed & Thu, noon–3:30pm & 6:30–11:30pm Fri & Sat ▪ www.geranium.dk ▪ ⓚⓚⓚ
Ranked as the second-best restaurant in the world after Noma in 2021, Geranium offers a truly unique meal with a focus on local seafood and quality ingredients. Booking is required at least 90 days in advance.

Entrance to Kong Hans Kælder

⑨ Kong Hans Kælder

This unique restaurant *(see p75)* is set in Copenhagen's oldest building, offering a wonderful atmosphere beneath its vaulted ceiling. Choose to eat from either the à la carte or fixed-price menu and watch the skilled chef at work in the open kitchen.

⑩ Søllerød Kro

This Michelin-star countryside inn *(see p105)* is a wonderful retreat away from the hubbub of central Copenhagen. The lovely interiors are matched by a standout menu that once more highlights the Danes' creative flair with flavours. A tasting menu is available with carefully chosen wine pairings.

TOP 10 DANISH CAFÉS AND BARS

The quirky Laundromat Café

1 Laundromat Café
MAP C3 ▪ Elmegade 15, Nørrebro
Enjoy a coffee while doing your laundry.

2 Coffee Collective
MAP H3 ▪ Vendersgade 6D
From farmer, to roaster, to barista, the Collective crafts the ultimate coffee.

3 Mad og Kaffe
MAP C6 ▪ Sønder Boulevard 68
The most popular café in the city is famous for colourful brunches.

4 Bo-Bi Bar
MAP J4 ▪ Klareboderne 4
Since 1917, artists and office drones have visited this tiny room to talk beer.

5 Café Dyrhaven
MAP C6 ▪ Sønder Boulevard 72
Café lattes and *smørrebrød* are the main offerings at this hip Vesterbro hangout.

6 Ruby
MAP J5 ▪ Nybrogade 10
One of the world's top 50 cocktail bars, situated on the canal.

7 La Glace
MAP H4 ▪ Skoubogade 3–5
La Glace is one of the foremost confectioneries in Copenhagen.

8 Kalaset
MAP D4 ▪ Vendersgade 16
A charming spot for hot chocolate with marshmellows and a vegetarian brunch.

9 Terroiristen
MAP B2 ▪ Jægersborggade 52
Organic, biodynamic wine processed with a focus on natural production, served with tapas or light meals.

10 Lidkoeb
MAP C5 ▪ Vesterbrogade 72B
Drinking den in a former apothecary; cocktail bar and whisky house.

For a key to restaurant price range see p75

Shopping Districts

1 Kronprinsensgade
MAP J4

This posh shopping area includes many of Scandinavia's top designer brands, such as Stig P and Le-Fix. You will also find Scandinavia's oldest tea shop, Perch's Tea Room.

2 Off Strøget (South)
MAP J4–J5

The streets to the south of Strøget are great for alternative shopping. Læderstræde and Kompagnistræde are especially good, the latter mostly for its antique shops.

3 Off Strøget (North)
MAP H4–J4

Heading up north from Strøget, you will find numerous little boutiques, record stores and second-hand shops. Go shopping on streets like Skindergade, Larsbjørnstræde, Vestergade and Studiestræde.

4 Strøget
MAP H5–K4

Copenhagen's shopping street is known as "the walking street". The shops, which stretch across five linked pedestrian streets, range from cheerful and inexpensive outlets to designer and upmarket department stores (towards Kongens Nytorv), with something for everyone.

Airy interior of the Fisketorvet mall

5 Fisketorvet Copenhagen Mall

MAP D6 ■ Kalvebod Brygge 59, Havneholmen 5, Vesterbro ■ 33 36 64 00 ■ Open 10am–8pm daily

On the waterfront facing the Inner Harbour, this city mall is minutes away from the Copencabana harbour pool. It has more than 120 shops, several restaurants and a cinema.

6 Vesterbro
MAP C5–C6

This former red-light area is now an offbeat shopping district offering some very good bargains. Among

Window-shopping along Copenhagen's famous shopping street, Strøget

the more interesting streets in the neighbourhood are Istedgade, which is lined with boutiques and art shops, and Værnedamsvej, which has several independent fashion stores and gourmet food shops.

7 Nansensgade
MAP G3

Located on the outskirts of the old town, this area has a mix of traditional and trendy boutiques, as well as good restaurants and cafés.

8 Torvehallerne KBH
MAP H3

Food-lovers sure are in for a treat at Copenhagen's covered market on Israels Plads. On offer here are a variety of gourmet food stands as well as takeout delights and some delicious delis.

Seafood stall at Torvehallerne KBH

9 Nørrebro
MAP C3–D3

Not as trendy as it once was, but Nørrebro still has many second-hand stores and chic boutiques. Head to Ravnsborggade for antiques, Jaegersborggade for the offbeat and Elmegade for vintage clothes.

10 Bredgade
MAP L3

If you are looking for traditional, pre-20th-century antiques, this is the perfect place to visit. Here you will find several grand-looking shops and auction houses that sell all kinds of antiques, including authentic paintings and statues.

TOP 10 DANISH DESIGN COMPANIES

Georg Jensen Silverware

1 Georg Jensen Silverware
www.georgjensen.com
Original, organic tableware designs and casual jewellery.

2 Cylinda-Line (by Arne Jacobsen)
www.stelton.dk
Popular tableware collection (1967) in steel, wood and plastic.

3 Bang & Olufsen
www.bang-olufsen.com
Known for their cutting-edge audio-visual designs.

4 Kaare Klint Furniture
Combines ergonomics with elegant 18th-century English styles.

5 Bodum
www.bodum.com
Classic and smart kitchenware in steel and glass.

6 LEGO®
www.lego.com
These popular building blocks were introduced in 1952.

7 Vipp
www.vipp.com
Designers of a classic stainless steel pedal bin, Vipp's products also include soap dishes and dispensers.

8 Royal Copenhagen
www.royalcopenhagen.com
Royal porcelain design featuring famous Flora Danica motifs.

9 Poul Henningsen Lamps
Lamp design creating the effect of maximum light and minimum shadow.

10 Kjærholm Furniture
Poul Kjærholm-designed functional coffee tables and chairs, all named simply PK with a number. Production continues under the leadership of his son, Thomas.

🔟 Copenhagen for Free

The Royal Botanical Gardens

1 Botanisk Have

Take a stroll through this green oasis *(see p78)* in the heart of the city, which has stunning glasshouses, gardens and over 13,000 species of plant life. Behind the scenes, the garden's botanists develop scientific collections of rare plants and fungi, making them available for research, teaching and the public.

2 World-class museums
www.natmus.dk

All of the city's national museums, including Nationalmuseet *(see pp32–3)* and the SMK – National Gallery of Denmark *(see pp26–7)*, are free for under-18s, while many city-centre institutions offer free entry for adults one day per week – check the relevant website for specific days.

3 Open-air movie
MAP D2 ■ Edel Sauntes Allé
■ www.zulu.dk

It doesn't get much more hygge (cosy) than this: every summer, Zulu, a Danish television station, brings its open-air cinema to venues around Copenhagen. All you need to do is bring a blanket and some snacks.

4 Havnebadet
MAP E6 ■ Islands Brygge 14
■ www.svoemkbh.kk.dk/en/node/14

On hot days, Copenhageners flock to this open-air swimming bath. There are five pools in all, while three diving towers give thrill-seekers the opportunity to show off their stunts.

5 A Harbourside Promenade

Make the obligatory visit to the Little Mermaid *(see p13)* on foot, and then continue inland into Kastellet, the historic green fortress that is still a working military barracks, before exploring the Gefion Fountain and St Alban's Church *(see p80)*.

6 Den Sorte Diamant
MAP K5 ■ Søren Kierkegaards Plads 1

Not only does this modern extension of the Royal Library house every book ever printed in Danish (some six million), it's also home to the very good National Museum of Photography.

7 Changing of the guard at Amalienborg Palace

Come rain or shine, the Royal Life Guards stoically stand watch outside Amalienborg Palace *(see pp24–5)*. Every day at noon, you can watch them march through the city.

8 Christiansborg Tårnet

At 106 m (348 ft), the tower on Christiansborg Palace *(see pp30–31)* is the highest point in the historic centre of Copenhagen, and offers great views of the city. Space on the viewing platform is limited, so expect to queue for the elevator.

9 Christiania

A maze of hippy hangouts and Hobbit-like homes, this self-declared "freetown" *(see pp28–9)* has been a counter-culture haven for dreamers and anarchists for more than 40 years.

Communal area in Christiania

10 Absalon

MAP C6 ■ Sønder Blvd 73 ■ Open 7:30am–midnight Sun–Thu (until 2am Fri & Sat) ■ www.absaloncph.dk

Play ping-pong, dance the tango or try some traditional Danish cooking at this free activity centre.

Changing of the Guard, Amalienborg Palace

TOP 10 BUDGET TIPS

A street food outlet in Copenhagen

1 Try street food
Fast-food outlets are plentiful, and street-food outlets offer substantial, high-quality dishes for 100 Dkr or less.

2 Have a big breakfast
Eat-all-you-want breakfasts offer good value for money, even at 100–150 Dkr.

3 Dine outside
Barbecues, picnics and alcohol are allowed in most public parks across Copenhagen, ideal for dining alfresco.

4 Get outdoors
The public parks (except Tivoli) are free and host free entertainment.

5 Free walking tours
Several walking tour operators that provide tips and sight information. A tip is expected at the end of tour.

6 See a free concert
MAP H5 ■ Vesterbrogade 3
Tivoli *(see p14)* has a summer concert series often with international artists. Free with park admission every Friday.

7 Free outdoor concerts
Every Wednesday in the spring and summer, students from the Royal Danish Academy of Music perform classical concerts at the Teatermuseet.

8 Buy a Copenhagen Card or a Copenhagen City Pass
Both cards offer sightseeing discounts. Copenhagen Card includes free public transportation as well *(see p108)*.

9 Don't worry about tipping
Tips are usually included in bills at restaurants, hotels and taxis.

10 Try ice-skating
Skate for free in winter at ice-skating rinks. Popular spots include Frederiksberg Runddel and Enghaveparken, but locations may vary.

Copenhagen
Area by Area

A view across the striking rooftops
of Copenhagen's old city

🔟 Tivoli North to Gothersgade

A fun ride at Tivoli

Rich in history and culture, this area is a popular entertainment destination. Heading northeast of Tivoli, which was originally outside the city walls, you can walk back in time through the old town that evolved during the Middle Ages – though much of it succumbed to fire in the 18th century – to Slotsholmen, the site where the first dwellings that became the city of Copenhagen were built in the 12th century. Along the way, you will find great shopping areas, museums, an old town Christian V Statue and a truly wonderful royal palace to explore.

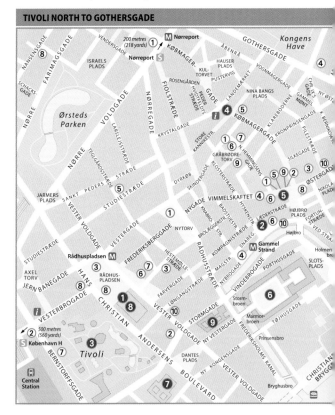

TIVOLI NORTH TO GOTHERSGADE

Astronomical clock on display

1 Astronomical Clock

MAP H5 ■ Rådhus, Rådhuspladsen 1 ■ 33 66 33 66 ■ Open 9:30am–4pm Mon–Fri, 9:30am–1pm Sat ■ Adm

This clock shows local time, solar time, sunrise and sunset times, celestial pole movement and the movement of the planets.

2 Kunstforeningen Gammel Strand

MAP J4 ■ Gammel Strand 48 ■ 33 36 02 60 ■ Open 11am–6pm Tue, Wed & Fri (until 8pm Thu), 11am–5pm Sat & Sun ■ Adm, free with Copenhagen City Pass ■ www.glstrand.dk

The Gammel Strand art association was formed in 1825. The centre puts on five to six changing exhibitions annually, from restrospectives to group shows, both classic and contemporary. There is an excellent bookshop as well as a café on the first floor. Visitors with specific requirements would need to pass through the courtyard at Læderstræde 15 for access.

3 Tivoli

A park that is now almost synonymous with Copenhagen, Tivoli (see pp14–15) is a must-visit. In any season, this park buzzes with the sounds of exhilarating rides. It is not only for adventure-seekers though. At night, the setting turns quite magical, with fairy lights and Japanese lanterns glowing in the darkness. There's often live music, too.

Beautiful lighting at Tivoli

4 Latin Quarter

To the west of Strøget lies the Latin Quarter (see pp18–19), the original home of the University of Copenhagen. It dates back to the Middle Ages when the primary language of education was Latin. Some of the old university buildings are used, although much of the campus is now on the island of Amager.

⑤ Amagertorv
MAP J4

This busy square is in the middle of Strøget. The square's focal point, the lovely Storkespringvandet fountain, provided the inspiration for a Danish folk song of the 1960s, and today the fountain is a popular meeting place. The cafés Norden and Europa, on either side of the square, are always buzzing. Note the attractive tiles designed by Bjørn Nørgaard.

Statues at Ny Carlsberg Glyptotek

⑥ Slotsholmen

A visit to Slotsholmen could take up almost an entire day, as there is plenty to see. It is primarily the site of Christiansborg Slot *(see pp30–31)*, which burnt down in 1794, but was rebuilt and is now home to Denmark's Parliament; it is also used for State functions by the Queen (visit the Royal Reception Rooms on a guided tour). Museums here include the Danish War Museum, filled with historic arms and armour, and the delightful Teatermuseet *(see p44)* featuring the 18th-century palace theatre. Other sights include the palace church and the 12th-century ruins of the first Copenhagen castle where the city's founder, Bishop Absalon, resided.

⑦ Ny Carlsberg Glyptotek
MAP H6 ■ **Dantes Plads 7** ■ **33 41 81 41** ■ **Open 10am–5pm Tue–Sun (until 9pm Thu)** ■ **Adm, free with Copenhagen City Pass, Tue free** ■ **www.glyptoteket.com**

This superb art gallery *(see p44)* is home to a diverse collection of Mediterranean, classical and Egyptian art and artifacts. Danish and 19th-century French artworks are also on display. The collection includes splendid French Impressionist paintings. The museum is housed in a 19th-century building with a cupola, beneath which lies an indoor winter garden, sculptures and water features. The modern wing is a wonderful area filled with light.

⑧ Rådhus
MAP H5 ■ **Rådhuspladsen 1** ■ **33 66 25 86** ■ **Open 9am–4pm Mon–Fri, 9:30am–1pm Sat** ■ **Tours in English at 1pm Mon–Fri, 10am Sat; tower tour 11am & 2pm Mon–Fri, noon Sat** ■ **Adm for tours and tower, free with Copenhagen Card**

A mock-Gothic building replete with fantastical sea creatures, The Rådhus, or town hall, was built between 1892 and 1905 and designed by architect Martin Nyrop. Its tower affords superb views. Take a tour, or just pop in to see the pre-Raphaelitesque entrance way, or the Italianate reception hall. Many Copenhageners get married here, so you may see several wedding parties on the town hall steps.

9 Nationalmuseet

The National Museum *(see pp32–3)* is housed inside a former royal residence from the 18th century. The exhibits trace Danish history, from ancient times to the present, including some amazing ethnographic collections. The most popular exhibits at the museum chart the history of Danes from the Ice Age to the Viking campaigns.

10 Kongens Nytorv and Nyhavn

At the top of Nyhavn stands Kongens Nytorv or the King's New Square *(see pp22–3)*, an area surrounded by 18th-century mansions that house upmarket department stores, banks and hotels. The square is flanked by a number of prominent institutions such as Charlottenborg Slot (now an exhibition space and home to the academy of art) and Det Kongelige Teater or Royal Theatre. Nyhavn (meaning "new harbour") is filled with restaurants, cafés and old sailing boats along the canal quayside. The atmosphere here has changed since the 1670s. When Hans Christian Andersen lived here, it was a red-light district. Today, it's a popular waterfront spot where the satisfying sound of a beer bottle popping open is never far away.

Copenhagen's Rådhus

▶ **MORNING**

Start your day's ramble at the **Ny Carlsberg Glyptotek**; don't miss the impressive Egyptian and Impressionist collections. Have an early lunch at the museum's charming Picnic café *(Dantes Plads 7)*.

AFTERNOON

After lunch, cross H C Andersen Boulevard and head to the **Nationalmuseet** to take one of the hour-long tours. Stroll to the end of Ny Vestergade until you reach Frederiks Kanal. Cross the bridge and spend some time at **Christiansborg Slot** *(see pp30–31)*. If you arrive by 1:30pm, pop into the stables, the **Teatermuseet** *(see p44)* and the ruins before taking a tour of the Royal Reception Rooms at 3pm. Then, walk back over the bridge and turn right onto Gammel Strand for afternoon snacks at one of the many cafés and restaurants, such as **Fiskerkone** *(see p41)*. Walk down Købmagergade via Højbro Plads, right up to **Rundetaarn** *(see pp18–19)*. If you are feeling energetic, hike to the top for a good view of the city. Heading back down, take a left on to **Strøget** *(see p62)* and keep walking until you reach **Kongens Nytorv and Nyhavn** – a perfect spot for an evening drink and supper at one of the quayside restaurants and bars. Instead of heading back via Strøget, take the less mainstream Læderstræde. Walk to Rådhuspladsen *(see p72)* and go across to Tivoli *(see p14–15)*. Spend your evening enjoying this famous park.

See map on pp68–9

The Best of the Rest

1 Caritas Springvandet
MAP H4 ■ Gammel Torv

Dating back to 1608, the Charity Fountain is one of the city's oldest.

2 Københavns Museum
MAP H5 ■ Stormgade 18 ■ Opening hours vary ■ Adm ■ www.cphmuseum.kk.dk

The City Museum takes visitors on a journey through urban history, from the original settlers to today.

Caritas Fountain

3 Rådhuspladsen
MAP H5

At the end of Strøget, the town hall square is one of the liveliest areas and a key location for events.

4 Strøget
MAP H5–K4

This is the name given to the five main, interconnected shopping streets (see p62) of Copenhagen.

5 Guinness World Records Museum
MAP K4 ■ Østergade 16 ■ 33 32 31 31 ■ Open 10am–5pm Sun–Thu (to 6pm Fri & Sat) ■ Adm (combined tickets available) ■ www.guinnessworld recordsmuseum.dk

As the name suggests, 500 Guinness World Records are on display here (see p52).

6 World of H C Andersen Museum
MAP H5 ■ Rådhuspladsen 57 ■ 33 32 31 31 ■ Open 11am–5pm Sun–Thu (to 6pm Fri & Sat) ■ Adm ■ www.ripleys.com/copenhagen

Scenes from Andersen's fairy tales can be found here, in addition to a few other memorabilia.

7 Grand Teatret
MAP H5 ■ Mikkel Bryggers Gade 8 ■ 33 15 16 11 ■ www.grandteatret.dk

A historic six-screen cinema with some incredibly comfy seats and an excellent café, the Grand Teatret is the film buffs' go-to place for international and art-house movies.

8 Statue of H C Andersen
MAP H5 ■ H C Andersens Boulevard

This bronze statue of the author by Henry Lukow-Nielsen dates from 1961.

9 Georg Jensen Museum
MAP J4 ■ Amagertorv 4 ■ 33 11 40 80 ■ Open 11am–6pm Mon–Sat, 10am–5pm Sun ■ www.georgjensen.com

The jewellery and homeware of the famous silversmith are on display at this wonderful museum.

10 Gammel Strand
MAP J4

This canalside street is home to one of the city's best flea markets, great restaurants, as well as the Kunstforeningen Gammel Strand (see p69), a lovely art museum. It is also a pick-up point for Stromma Canal Tours (see pp12–13).

People enjoying a Stromma Canal Tour

Shops

1 Illums Bolighus
MAP J4 ■ Amagertorv 10 ■ 33
14 19 41 ■ www.illumsbolighus.dk
This shrine to stylish interior design
and kitchenware (mainly Italian and
Danish) offers everything from Royal
Copenhagen porcelain to groovy dog-
biscuit dispensers and objets d'art.

2 Georg Jensen
MAP J4 ■ Amagertorv 4 ■ 33
11 40 80 ■ www.georgjensen.com
Superb designs from the historic
firm of George Jensen are available
at its flagship store. These include a
range of stylish jewellery, watches,
cutlery, candlesticks, antiques and
designer sunglasses.

3 ILLUM
MAP K4 ■ Østergade 52
■ 33 14 40 02 ■ www.illum.dk
A stylish, six-storeyed department
store offering quality clothing and
homeware. There are also several
cafés, a bakery and a supermarket.

4 Stine Goya
MAP K3 ■ Gothersgade 58
■ www.stinegoya.com
A contemporary Danish fashion
brand, Stine Goya is famous for
its bold and colourful designs.

5 Royal Copenhagen Porcelain
MAP J4 ■ Amagertorv
6 ■ 33 13 71 81 ■ www.
royalcopenhagen.com
This flagship store offers a
range of designs, from the
classic 18th-century *flora
danica* design to the
modern and organic.

**A Royal Copenhagen
porcelain fruit bowl**

6 Mads Nørgaard
MAP J4 ■ Amagertov 15
■ 33 32 01 39 ■ www.madsnor
gaard.com
Classic, casual Danish menswear
is sold here, including the timeless
trademark unisex striped top.

7 Noa Noa
MAP K4 ■ Østergade 6
■ 35 42 23 22 ■ www.noanoa.com
A contemporary Danish label that
offers women's cottons, linens and
silks in quirky, pretty styles. They
also do a similar collection for
girls aged between 3–12.

Accessories on display at Hay House

8 Hay House
MAP J4 ■ Østergade 61, 2nd
Floor ■ 31 64 61 33 ■ www.hay.dk
Danish interior design store known
for its unique approach to furniture
and design pieces, which are often
crafted in unconventional shapes.

9 Apair
MAP K4
■ Ny Østergade 3
■ 33 91 99 20
■ www.apair.dk
Here you will find
fashionable footwear
for men and women, as well
as leather bags and belts
with large silver buckles.
It is a chain with shops
all over Denmark.

10 Sand
MAP K4
■ Østergade 40 ■ 33 14 21 21
■ www.sand-europe.com
This Danish fashion house offers
stylish and classic clothing and
accessories for men and women.

See map on pp68–9

Nightlife

The stylish Hard Rock Café at night

1 Hard Rock Café
MAP H5 ■ Rådhuspladsen 45–47
■ 33 12 43 33 ■ Opening hours vary
■ www.hardrock.com

This international chain has live music and features memorabilia from artists such as Metallica, The Rolling Stones, Amy Winehouse and Michael Jackson

2 Jernbanecafeen
MAP G6 ■ Reventlowsgade 16
■ 33 21 60 90 ■ Open 7am–2am daily

Located close to the Central Station, this is an old-fashioned Danish pub.

3 Taphouse
MAP H5 ■ Lavendelstræde
15 ■ Opening hours vary, check
website ■ www.taphouse.dk

An accessible beer bar offering a wide selection of pours at affordable prices.

4 Ruby
MAP J5 ■ Nybrogade 10 ■ 33
93 12 03 ■ Open 4pm–2am Mon–Thu
(from 3pm Fri & Sat) ■ www.rby.dk

This exclusive cocktail bar is located in an old townhouse from 1740.

5 Studenterhuset
MAP J3 ■ Købmagergade 52
■ Opening hours vary ■ www.
studenterhuset.com

A popular bar serving beer at discounted prices, Studenterhuset also hosts local bands.

6 The Jane
MAP J4 ■ Gråbrødretorv 8
■ 53 66 37 13 ■ Open from 8pm
Thu–Sat ■ www.thejane.dk

Step into a Mad Men-esque world at this city-centre speakeasy.

7 Strøm
MAP J4 ■ Niels Hemmingsens
Gade 32 ■ Open 4pm–2am Mon–Sat
■ www.strombar.dk

A spit 'n' sawdust speakeasy, Strøm serves up twists on classic cocktails.

8 Proud Mary Pub
MAP G5 ■ Vesterbrogade 2A
■ Opening hours vary, check website
■ www.proudmarypub.dk

Enjoy live music each night with a variety of beers and cocktails.

9 1105
MAP K4 ■ Kristen Bernikows
Gade 4 ■ 33 93 11 05 ■ Open
6pm–2am Wed, Thu & Sat (until
2am Fri) ■ www.1105.dk

At this modern and stylish bar, friendly staff serves skillfully crafted top-quality cocktails.

10 Club Mambo
MAP H5 ■ Vester Voldgade
85 ■ 33 11 97 66 ■ Open 9pm–
midnight Sun–Wed, 10pm–5am
Thu–Sat

Dance to salsa and bachata in this popular city-centre club.

See map on pp68–9

Places to Eat

PRICE CATEGORIES
For a three-course meal for one without alcohol, including taxes and charges.
....
ⓚ under 300 Dkr   ⓚⓚ 300–500 Dkr
ⓚⓚⓚ over 500 Dkr

1 Aamann's 1921
MAP J4 ■ Niels Hemmingsens Gade 19–21 ■ 20 80 52 04 ■ Open noon–5pm Mon–Sun, 6:30–10pm Tue–Sat ■ www.aamanns.dk/ aamanns-1921 ■ ⓚⓚ
Rooted in traditional Danish fare, Aamann's *(see p60)* offers an innovative interpretation of the classic Danish *smørrebrød*.

Smorgasbord at Aamann's 1921

2 L'Alsace
MAP K4 ■ Ny Østergade 9 ■ 33 14 57 43 ■ Open 11:30am–midnight Mon–Sat (except public hols) ■ www.alsace.dk ■ ⓚⓚ
This classy restaurant specializes in dishes from Alsace, especially fresh fish and seafood.

3 Kong Hans Kælder
MAP K4 ■ Vingårdsstræde 6 ■ 33 11 68 68 ■ Open 6pm–midnight Wed–Sat D ■ www.konghans.dk ■ ⓚⓚⓚ
Housed in the city's oldest building, this restaurant serves gourmet food in a formal setting.

4 Restaurant Llama
MAP K4 ■ Lille Kongensgade 14 ■ 89 93 66 87 ■ Open 5:30pm–midnight ■ www.cofoco.dk/en/llama/ ■ ⓚⓚ
Tasty Latin cuisine with a Nordic touch served in dimly lit surroundings.

5 Atlas Bar
MAP H4 ■ Larsbjørnsstræde 18 ■ 33 14 95 15 ■ Open noon–10pm Mon–Sat ■ www.atlasbar.dk ■ ⓚ
Locals head to this cool basement for a wide range of global dishes.

6 Krogs Fiskerestaurant
MAP J4 ■ Gammel Strand 38 ■ 33 15 89 15 ■ Open 11:30am–midnight Mon–Sat ■ www.krogs.dk ■ ⓚⓚ
This landmark fish restaurant offers organic and sustainable lunch menus.

7 Tivoli Food Hall
MAP H5 ■ Vesterbrogade 3 ■ 33 15 10 01 ■ Opening hours vary, check website ■ www.tivoli.dk ■ ⓚ
The food stalls here offer international dining experiences.

8 Bankeråt
MAP G3 ■ Ahlefeldtsgade 29 ■ 33 93 69 88 ■ Open 10:30am–11pm Mon–Tue (until midnight Wed–Sat & 8pm Sun) ■ www.bankeraat.dk ■ ⓚ
Enjoy steaks, salads and beers in this artistic venue.

9 Restaurant Peder Oxe
MAP J4 ■ Gråbrødretov 11 ■ 33 11 00 77 ■ Open noon–11pm Wed–Sat ■ www.pederoxe.dk ■ ⓚⓚ
A well-established restaurant on a picturesque square.

10 Kompasset
MAP L4 ■ Nyhavn 65 ■ 45 22 52 22 ■ Opening hours vary, check website ■ https://restaurant kompasset.dk ■ ⓚⓚ
This restaurant specializes in *smørrebrød* and offers harbour views.

Outdoor seating at Kompasset

TOP 10 Nørrebro, Østerbro and North of Gothersgade

Of these three neighbourhoods, two are additions to the original Copenhagen site, which took up what is now called the "Inner City". Until the 19th century, this area was mainly farmland; today it is a lively, multicultural part of the city with plenty of bars, cafés and alternative shopping centres. Østerbro, slightly northeast of Nørrebro, has remained an uncluttered, suburban residential area since the 19th century. The area north of Gothersgade is part of the Inner City and comprises parts of the capital that date back to the Renaissance period.

Vase from the Designmuseum

NØRREBRO, ØSTERBRO AND NORTH OF GOTHERSGADE

1 **Top 10 Sights**
see pp77–9

1 **Places to Eat**
see p83

1 **Shops**
see p81

1 **The Best of the Rest**
see p80

1 **Nightlife**
see p82

1 Assistens Kirkegård

MAP C3 ■ Kapelvej ■ 33 66 91 00 ■ Open 7am–10pm daily (Oct–Mar: until 7pm) ■ www.assistens.dk

If you are not a devoted fan of famous dead Danes, this cemetery may not be top of your list. However, it is a wonderful place to relax or take a romantic walk. The church-yard is beautiful and is located in the Nørrebro district.

2 Marmorkirken

Standing close to Amalienborg is the splendid Marmorkirken or Marble Church *(see pp24–5)*, a part of the great architectural design for the area of Frederiksstaden. However, plans for its construction were so extravagant that finances ran out

The splendid Marmorkirken cupola

and work was abandoned in 1770. For more than a century, it stood as a picturesque ruin before being rescued and financed by a Danish industrialist, and in 1894 the church was finally completed.

3 Amalienborg

Some royal palaces allow visits only during summer week-ends. Amalienborg (both Christian VII and Christian VIII's Palaces) and the museum are open to the public year-round. The palaces were built as an important part of the 18th-century aristocratic district Frederiksstaden *(see pp24–5)* and are very different from the narrow streets and houses of the old quarter. Amalienborg is a stone's throw away from the Marble Church *(see p25)* and offers peerless views of the modern Opera House *(see p95)* across the harbour – a stark architectural contrast to these Rococo confines.

Amalienborg royal palace

The popular, well-manicured gardens of Botanisk Have

④ Botanisk Have

MAP H2–J2 ■ Gothersgade 128 ■ Open Apr–Sep: 8:30am–6pm daily; Oct–Mar: 8:30am–4pm daily ■ Adm, free entrance to the garden ■ www.botanik.snm.ku.dk

Among the prettiest outdoor spaces in Copenhagen, these gardens (see p64) are studded with lakes, bridges and flowerbeds. Climb the winding staircase for a great view of exotic trees below. In 2024, the grounds will house the Natural History Museum of Denmark, which will merge two of its currently separate entities into one state-of-the-art building.

⑤ Davids Samling

MAP K3 ■ Kronprinsessegade 30–32 ■ 33 73 49 49 ■ Open 10am–5pm Tue–Sun (until 9pm Wed) ■ www.davidmus.dk

This museum holds the private art collection of Danish Supreme Court barrister C L David. The Islamic collection is Scandinavia's largest, and includes a fine range of Islamic art from the 7th to the 19th centuries. There is also a collection of 18th- and 19th-century European decorative arts, including a collection of early modern Danish art from 1880–1950.

Statue at Rosenborg Slot

⑥ Den Hirschsprungske Samling

MAP J1 ■ Stockholmsgade 20 ■ 35 42 03 36 ■ Open 11am–4pm Wed–Sun (until 8pm last Thu of the month) ■ Adm ■ www.hirschsprung.dk

This small art museum is situated just behind the SMK and displays the collection that was given to the nation in 1902 by the tobacco magnate, Heinrich Hirschsprung. Housed in a 19th-century building, the large collection is fittingly dedicated to 19th- and early 20th-century Danish art, including works by painters from the North Jutland colony of Skagen, who are known for their bright colours and luminous treatment of light. Contemporary furniture is also displayed in the museum.

⑦ Rosenborg Slot and Kongens Have

Rosenborg Castle and the King's Garden (see pp16–17) are among the highlights of the city, especially on sunny days when the park is full of people and entertainment. Rosenborg Slot was built in 1606–34 and is the only castle in the city centre that has not succumbed to fire. Little has changed about the structure since the time the royals inhabited it in the 17th century.

8 Frihedsmuseet

MAP L2 ■ Esplanaden 13
■ 41 20 60 80 ■ Open May–Aug:
10am–5pm daily; Sep–Apr: 10am–
5pm Tue–Sun ■ www.natmus.dk

The Museum of Danish Resistance
pays tribute to, and tells the stories
of, the people who lived in Denmark
during German occupation (1940–45).
It explores their resistance activities,
from underground newspapers
and radio stations to sabotage and
the rescue of virtually every Jew
in Denmark. Group tours exploring
different aspects of occupied life
are also available.

9 SMK – National Gallery of Denmark

The SMK *(see pp26–7)* has collections
of both national and international art,
including works by the Old Masters
and modern icons.

A painting at the SMK

10 Designmuseum Danmark

MAP L2 ■ Bredgade 68 ■ 33 18 56
56 ■ Open 10am–6pm Tue–Sun
(until 9pm Wed) ■ Adm, free with
Copenhagen Card ■ www.design
museum.dk

Dedicated entirely to the art of design,
this museum *(see p44)* is housed in a
splendid 18th-century Rococo building.
The collection comprises everything
from Danish-designed colanders and
cardboard chairs to posters, textiles
and Chinese decorative arts.

A WALK NORTH OF GOTHERSGADE

▶ MORNING

Start your day among the
Impressionistic paintings of the
Danish Skagen colony of painters
at the **Den Hirschsprungske
Samling** museum. Then cross
the gardens to the impressive
**SMK – National Gallery of
Denmark**; take an audio guide
to learn about the displays.

AFTERNOON

For lunch, stop at either the
museum café or the **Botanisk
Have** café, depending upon the
weather. The gardens are a great
place for a picnic, too. Don't forget
to visit the Palm House. Heading
out from the gate on Gothersgade
turn onto Øster Voldgade, cross
over to **Rosenborg Slot**. Spend a
few enjoyable hours here, visiting
the castle, the crown jewels and
strolling through the gardens.

Afterwards leave from the
Kronprinsessegade gate and
pop into **Davids Samling** to see
some Islamic art. Amble down
Dronningens Tværgade, take a
left onto Bredgade and walk right
up to **Marmorkirken** *(see p77)*. If
you are here after 1pm, take a tour
up the tower. Right in front of the
church is **Amalienborg** *(see p77)*.
Take a walk through it to the
pretty banks of the harbour and
see the **Opera House** *(see p94)*
across the water. If you are up for
a 20-minute walk, head towards
The Little Mermaid *(see p80)*,
passing **Gefionspringvandet**
(see p80) and **Frihedsmuseet**.
To get back to town, hop onto
the No. 26 bus from Folke
Bernadottes Allé.

See map on pp76–7

The Best of the Rest

1 Gefionspringvandet
MAP M2 ▪ Langelinie

This bronze statue is a dramatic sight, representing the tale of the goddess Gefion as she ploughs enough land to create the island of Zealand, on which Copenhagen is found.

The bronze statue of goddess Gefion

2 Medicinsk Museion
MAP L2 ▪ Bredgade 62 ▪ 35 32 38 00 ▪ Open 10am–4pm Mon–Fri, noon–4pm Sat & Sun ▪ Guided tour in English 2pm Tue–Fri, 1:30pm Sat & Sun ▪ Adm ▪ www.museion.ku.dk

The Medical Museum of Copenhagen University has exhibits dating back to the 18th century.

3 The Little Mermaid (Den Lille Havfrue)
MAP M1 ▪ Langelinie, top of Kastellet

This statue of the heroine of Hans Christian Andersen's fairy tale, *The Little Mermaid (see p13)*, perched on a rock in the harbour, has been staring out to sea since 1913.

4 Amaliehaven
Filled with box hedges and fountains, this modern park *(see p24)* lies to the east of Amalienborg, facing the harbour, with views of the Opera House.

5 Alexander Nevsky Kirke
MAP L3 ▪ Bredgade 53 ▪ 29 61 39 08 ▪ Opening hours vary, call ahead

This Russian Orthodox church (1883) was a gift from Tsar Alexander III to celebrate his marriage to the Danish Princess Marie Dagmar.

6 Kastelskirken
MAP L1 ▪ Kastellet ▪ 21 31 00 28 ▪ Open 8am–6pm Mon–Fri

The military church at Kastellet has been holding services here since the 18th century.

7 St Alban's Church
MAP M2 ▪ Churchillparken 11 ▪ 39 62 77 36 ▪ Open summer: 10am–4pm Mon–Fri ▪ www.st-albans.dk

St Alban's is Denmark's only Anglican church and is a Neo-Gothic building dating from 1885.

8 Kongelige Afstøbningssamling
MAP M2 ▪ Toldbodgade 40 ▪ 33 74 84 84 ▪ Open for special events ▪ www.smk.dk

The Royal Cast Collection is heralded on the harbour with a replica of Michelangelo's statue of *David*.

9 Fælledparken
MAP D2

Copenhagen's largest park *(see p53)* is where the city gathers for the annual springtime celebrations on 1 May.

10 Kastellet
MAP L1 ▪ 72 81 11 41 ▪ Only grounds open to visitors

This pentagram-shaped fortress was constructed as a protective measure against the Swedes, but was only ever used against the English in 1807.

A cannon on show at Kastellet

Shops

1 Nyhavns Glaspusteri
MAP L4 ■ Toldbodgade 4
■ 40 17 01 34 ■ www.copenhagen
glass.dk
This charming glass gallery is where glass-blower Christian Edwards sculpts and sells his creations.

2 Divaen og Krudtuglen
MAP C3 ■ Elmegade 22
■ 26 71 59 68 ■ www.millou.dk
Bright clothes and shoes for kids and mums alike, as well as trays of cute, inexpensive toys. Look out for the ecofriendly labelled brands.

3 Prag Nørrebro
MAP C3 ■ Nørrebrogade
45 ■ 33 21 00 50 ■ www.prag
copenhagen.com
This popular second-hand clothes shop draws inspiration from New York and Berlin's vintage fashion scenes.

4 Tage Andersen Boutique & Museum
MAP K4 ■ Ny Adelgade 12 ■ 33 93 09 13 ■ Adm ■ www.tage-andersen.com
Run by flower artist and designer Tage Andersen, this flower shop, gallery and museum is full of lovely and unique arrangements. To see the whole place you'll need to climb up a steep staircase.

5 Ecouture
MAP J4 ■ Gråbrødretorv 7
■ 71 79 01 01 ■ www.ecouture.com
One of the pioneering sustainable fashion shops in the city, Ecouture offers well-crafted theatrical and vintage designs.

6 Brund
MAP E2 ■ Nordre Frihavnsgade 49 ■ 35 43 51 33 ■ www.brund.dk
Raw denim and bench-made boots line the shelves of this rugged menswear shop, which stocks a selection of high-end goods from brands including Loake, John Smedley and Crockett & Jones.

Interior of Normann Copenhagen

7 Normann Copenhagen
MAP E2 ■ Østerbrogade 70
■ 35 55 44 59 ■ www.normann-copenhagen.com
This vast warehouse set in an old cinema sells designer furniture, clothes and interior design items.

8 Hooha
MAP C3 ■ Elmegade 14
■ 35 37 60 37 ■ www.hooha.dk
A stylish little store, Hooha sells clothes and accessories for all, but caters mostly to men.

9 Le Fix
MAP J4 ■ Kronprinsensgade 9 ■ 88 82 37 81
A menswear boutique with roots in underground art movements, Le Fix offers a wide range of hoodies, denims and oversized T-shirts.

10 Mondo Kaos
MAP C3 ■ Birkegade 1 ■ 60 95 11 36 ■ www.mondokaos.dk
New versions of vintage clothes, including retro 1950s-style dresses, are on the racks of this colourful rockabilly boutique.

See map on pp76–7

Nightlife

① BRUS
MAP C3 ▪ Guldbergsgade 29F
▪ 75 22 22 00 ▪ www.tapperietbrus.dk

With 32 draft beers and an in-house bottleshop, there's plenty to keep even the thirstiest beer lover interested at this Nørrebro brewpub.

The elegant BRUS bar

② Chateau Motel
MAP D5 ▪ Knabrostræde 3 ▪ 53 89 31 34 ▪ www.chateaumotel.dk

At Chateau Motel (see p57), different genres of music are played across its four storeys. It is counted among Copenhagen's biggest nightclubs.

③ Kassen
MAP D3 ▪ Nørrebrogade 18B
▪ 71 92 92 18 ▪ www.kassen.dk

A cocktail bar with the look, feel and pricing of a typical Dutch pub. Kassen also has a small dance floor.

④ The Barking Dog
MAP D3 ▪ Sankt Hans Gade 19 ▪ 35 36 16 00 ▪ www.thebarking dog.dk

A hit with students and hipsters alike, this wallet-friendly cocktail bar is where mixologists spin classic funk and soul records while they create the drinks.

⑤ Empire Bio Cinema
MAP C3 ▪ Guldbergsgade 29F ▪ 35 36 00 36
▪ www.empirebio.dk

This comfortable cinema holds good programmes and has a cosy bar and café area.

⑥ Søernes Ølbar
MAP E2 ▪ Sortedam Dossering 83 ▪ 32 19 63 80 ▪ www.soernes oelbar.dk

A lakeside craft-beer joint with an impeccable selection of draft and bottled ales, porters and sours, this is a haven for hopheads on the hunt for rare and obscure brews.

⑦ DuPong
MAP C4 ▪ Griffenfeldsgade 52
▪ www.dupong.dk

Cheap beer and table football make this cosy little bar a must-visit for pub sports enthusiasts.

⑧ JOJO Vesterbro
MAP B5 ▪ Sundevedsgade 4
▪ Open 4pm–midnight Mon–Sat
▪ www.jojovesterbro.dk

A favourite among the locals, JOJO Vesterbro is an accessible bar offering cheap, top-quality cocktails in a great atmosphere.

⑨ Mexibar
MAP C3 ▪ Elmegade 27
▪ 35 37 77 66 ▪ www.mexibar.dk

This cosy, Mexican-inspired bar serves good cocktails. The staff create a friendly atmosphere.

⑩ Rust
MAP C3 ▪ Guldbergsgade 8
▪ 35 24 52 00 ▪ Open 8:30pm–5am Fri & Sat ▪ www.rust.dk

Tune into Copenhagen's alternative live music scene at this bar (see p56), spread over three floors.

The bar and booths at Rust

Places to Eat

① Orangeriet Kongens Have

MAP K3 ■ Kronprinsessegade 13 ■ Open 11:30am–3pm Mon–Fri, 6–11pm Thu–Sat, smørrebrød menu: noon–4pm Sun ■ www. restaurant-orangeriet.dk ■ Ⓚ Ⓚ

This orangery in the park offers open sandwiches and light seasonal dishes.

Interior of Orangeriet Kongens Have

② Møntergade

MAP J3 ■ Gammel Mønt 41 ■ 33 33 06 10 ■ Open 11:30am–5pm & 6–11pm daily ■ www.montergade. dk ■ Ⓚ

Excellent *smørrebrød* are on offer here, with an array of toppings.

③ Restaurant Zeleste

MAP L4 ■ Store Strandstræde 6 ■ 33 16 06 06 ■ Open noon–10pm daily (until 10:30pm Fri & Sat) ■ www. zeleste.dk ■ Ⓚ Ⓚ

A restaurant with a cosy interior, Zeleste serves elegant Danish dishes.

④ Kiin Kiin

MAP C3 ■ Guldbergsgade 21 ■ 35 35 75 55 ■ Open 5:30pm–midnight Mon–Sat ■ www.kiin.dk ■ Ⓚ Ⓚ Ⓚ

Thai street food meets inventive fusion cooking at this restaurant *(see p60)*.

⑤ Bæst

MAP C3 ■ Guldbergsgade 29 ■ 35 35 04 63 ■ www.baest.dk ■ Ⓚ

Enjoy charcuterie, cheeses and wood-fired pizzas at this diner.

⑥ Ramen To Biiru

MAP C3 ■ Griffenfeldsgade 28 ■ 50 53 02 22 ■ www. ramentobiiru.dk ■ Ⓚ

A quirky craft beer and noodle bar, Ramen To Biiru has a retrofuturistic vending machine where you place your order.

⑦ Salt Bar and Restaurant

MAP L3 ■ Toldbodgade 24–28 ■ 33 74 14 44 ■ Open daily ■ www. saltrestaurant.dk ■ Ⓚ Ⓚ

In an 18th-century granary, this bar and restaurant serves cocktails and French-Danish cuisine.

⑧ Gro Spiseri

MAP D1 ■ Æbeløgade 4 ■ Closed Jan & Feb; open 5:30–11pm Mon, Thu, Fri (from 10am Sat & Sun) ■ www.grospiseri.dk ■ Ⓚ Ⓚ

This rooftop urban farm and restaurant serves organic food with a focus on sustainability. Book ahead.

⑨ Fischer

MAP E2 ■ Victor Borges Plads 12 ■ 35 42 39 64 ■ Open 5–11pm Wed–Sat ■ www.hosfischer.dk ■ Ⓚ Ⓚ

A tiny Italian restaurant, Fischer is a favourite with local restaurant critics.

⑩ Kate's Joint

MAP C4 ■ Blågårdsgade 12 ■ 35 37 44 96 ■ Open 5–10pm Mon–Wed (until 10:30pm Thu & 11pm Sat) ■ Relish a variety of vegetarian and vegan dishes with Malay, Middle Eastern and Indian influences.

See map on pp76–7 ←

🔟 Vesterbro and Frederiksberg

Vesterbro and Frederiksberg lie side by side to the southwest and west of the Inner City. In the 19th century, both areas were outside the city walls; this was when Tivoli was built on Vesterbro's edge. Vesterbro formerly included a red-light district, and many poorer residents lived in humble flats with no running water. Although the area retains an edginess shared only by the Nørrebro district, much of it has now  been regenerated. Today, you will find a rich and thriving culture, restaurants, bars and designer outlets. In contrast, the prosperous Frederiksberg is an upmarket residential area.

An exhibit at Visit Carlsberg

VESTERBRO AND FREDERIKSBERG

Previous pages The chapel at Frederiksberg Slot

Tycho Brahe Planetarium exterior

1 Tycho Brahe Planetarium
MAP C5 ■ Gammel Kongevej 10 ■ 33 12 12 24 ■ Open noon–6pm Mon, 9:30am–8pm Tue–Wed (until 8:30pm Thu–Sat, 7pm Sun) ■ Adm, free with Copenhagen City Pass ■ www.tycho.dk

The permanent exhibition at the planetarium includes displays on the natural sciences, astronomy and space travel. However, one of the biggest attractions is the IMAX cinema; visitors are blown away by the high-quality images on the 1,000-sq-m (10,760-sq-ft) dome screen. Films shown here cover topics such as astronomy and space research, and virtually transport you to another world. The minimum age for the film audience is 3 years.

2 Frederiksberg Slot
MAP A5 ■ Roskildevej 28A ■ 72 81 77 71

Set in Frederiksberg Have, one of the most romantic spots in Copenhagen, this Baroque-style palace was the royal family's summer residence until the mid-1800s. It's perched on a park hilltop, surrounded by many lovely little bridges, and the Chinese Pavilion that was erected in 1799 as a royal teahouse. It now houses the Danish Officer's Academy and is only open for guided tours.

3 Frederiksberg Have
MAP A5 ■ Frederiksberg Runddel ■ 33 95 42 00 ■ Open 6am–7pm daily

Surrounding Frederiksberg Slot, this park is one of the city's loveliest green areas. Between 1798 and 1802, the original Baroque gardens were landscaped to conform with the Romantic style of the English garden. Several buildings here date back to the early 19th century, including the Chinese Pavilion and the Apis Temple.

The sprawling Frederiksberg Have

4 Visit Carlsberg

MAP A6 ▪ Gamle Carlsberg Vej 11 ▪ 33 27 10 20 ▪ Opening hours vary, check website ▪ Adm, under-6s free ▪ www.visitcarlsberg.dk

A legendary landmark, this is the place where the famous brewery was founded back in 1847, growing beyond its local roots and transforming into a world-renowned power brand. A treat for all senses, this offers the smell of beer ingredients, the sight of outstanding architecture, songs of old brewers and of course a taste of the beer itself. It is currently closed for remodeling. Visitors can opt for a self-guided tour or take the help of the experienced guides, to know more about the place once it is open.

5 Zoologisk Have

MAP A5 ▪ Roskildevej 32 ▪ 72 20 02 00 ▪ Opening hours vary, check website ▪ Adm ▪ www.zoo.dk

Situated close to the Frederiksborg Slot, the Zoologisk Have is open 365 days a year and makes for a lovely day out. It is one of the oldest zoos in Europe. Here you will find a wide variety of animals, from tigers and giraffes to hippos, elephants as well as monkeys (including tiny, endangered Golden Lion Tamarins). You can also see a variety of butterflies and birds in the tropical section. Make sure you visit the Arctic Ring exhibit, which gives you a unique opportunity to get closer to the magnificent polar bears, North Atlantic birds and seals.

Interior of the Cisternerne

6 Cisternerne – The Cisterns

MAP A6 ▪ Søndermarken ▪ 30 73 80 32 ▪ Opening hours vary, check website ▪ Adm, under-18s free ▪ www.cisternerne.dk

Once the subterranean water reservoir of the city, this space is now famous for contemporary art exhibitions. The dimly lit 19th-century dripstone cave is immense, engulfing and slightly spooky; the art experience, though, is guaranteed to be magical.

7 Radisson Collection Royal Hotel, Copenhagen

This 20-storey tower-block hotel, designed by architect Arne Jacobsen, represents the cutting-edge design style of the 1950s. The hotel *(see p116)* is littered with his iconic Egg and Swan chairs.

Elegant interiors of the Radisson Collection Royal Hotel, Copenhagen

8 **Sønder Boulevard**
MAP C6

Following its transformation into a long, green belt in 2007, Sønder Boulevard is one of Vesterbro's most popular recreational areas and hang-out spots. The area is filled with shops and great cafés. There is also artificial grass for ball games and a number of playgrounds.

9 **Bakkehuset**
MAP B6 ■ Rahbeks Allé 23, Frederiksberg ■ Open 11am–6pm Tue–Fri (until 5pm Sat & Sun) ■ Adm ■ www.bakkehusmuseet.dk

Formerly the home of 19th-century literary personalities Knud Lyne and Kamma Rahbek, this house is now a cultural museum. The ground floor has the Fairytale Academy – a homage to the friendship between Rahbek and Hans Christian Andersen, who visited Bakkehuset as a young man. Here, Andersen found inspiration to pursue his dream of becoming a writer.

A room at Bakkehuset

10 **Storm P. Museet**
MAP A5 ■ Frederiksberg Runddel ■ 38 86 05 00 ■ Open 11am–6pm Tue–Fri (until 5pm Sat & Sun) ■ Adm, free with Copenhagen City Pass ■ www.stormp.dk

This small and delightful museum is dedicated to the whimsical and satirical wit of the Danish cartoonist Storm P. His work is reminiscent of the social realism of the late 19th and early 20th centuries, such as the styles of Daumier and Degas. The humour comes through in the dialogues of his characters and if you speak Danish, you will derive great enjoyment from these cartoons.

A WALK AROUND VESTERBRO

▶ MORNING

Start at the city's **central station**, Hovedbanegård, and admire the Frihedsstøtten or "pillar of freedom" (1792). Continue down Vesterbrogade and take a left at Reventlowgade, then take a right onto Istedgade. Walk up to Halmtorvet, a former cattle market now full of cafés, known as Den Brune Kødby ("brown meat city"). The building opposite is Øksnehallen, Vesterbro's biggest cultural exhibition space. Stroll to the blue-painted complex, **Den Hvide Kødby** ("white meat city"), now a lively cluster of bars and galleries. Head back to Halmtorvet, walk on and take a right on Skydebanegade. At the end of the street is a wall that protected inhabitants from shooting practice in the gardens on the other side. Enter the gate in the wall, turn left and walk through the park on your right to Vesterbrogade. Turn left and walk down the street, taking a left onto Oehlenschlægersgade, where you will find the extraordinary building, **Mosaic**, created by the late Nigerian-born artist Manuel Tafat.

AFTERNOON

Head back to Vesterbrogade for lunch at **Les Trois Cochons** (see p91), or continue down Oehlenschlægersgade until you reach the trendy bars and boutiques on Istedgade. You could also stop for lunch or a drink at **Café Bang & Jensen** (see p91). Spend the rest of the afternoon browsing in the stylish shops.

See map on pp86–7 ←

Shopping

Bicycles parked outside a coffee lounge on Værnedamsvej

1 Kyoto
MAP C6 ▪ Istedgade 95 ▪ 33 31 66 36 ▪ www.kyoto.dk

This store has fashionable wear from Scandinavian and French brands for both men and women, as well as a substantial collection of sneakers.

2 Donn Ya Doll
MAP C5 ▪ Istedgade 55 ▪ 33 22 66 35 ▪ Open 10am–6pm Mon–Fri, 11am–4pm Sat

Donn Ya Doll opened in the 1990s and stocks original accessories and clothing, some designed by the owner.

3 Girlie Hurly
MAP C6 ▪ Istedgade 99 ▪ 42 49 22 41 ▪ Open 11am–5:30pm Mon–Fri, 10:30am–3pm Sat

This shop is filled with quirky items ranging from bags and candles to lamps and crockery.

4 Rockahula
MAP C6 ▪ Istedgade 91 ▪ 26 23 34 67 ▪ www.rockahula.dk

An intriguing boutique dedicated to all things 1950s and rockabilly, Rockahula also has a children's line.

5 Heidi & Bjarne
MAP C6 ▪ Istedgade 85 ▪ www.heidiogbjarne.dk

Here, you will find clothes for newborns to 12-year-olds. Proceeds are donated to Settlementet, a nonprofit.

6 Værnedamsvej
MAP C5

A gourmet food street, this place has wine and chocolate shops, butchers and fishmongers and more.

7 Edison & Co.
MAP C6 ▪ Sønder Boulevard 39 ▪ 61 67 26 94 ▪ www.edisonogco.dk

If you are looking for souvenirs, this store offers a variety of furniture and other decorative items for interiors.

8 Meyers Deli
MAP B5 ▪ Gammel Kongevej 107 ▪ 33 25 45 95 ▪ Open until 9pm daily ▪ www.meyersdeli.dk

Claus Meyer helped kickstart the Nordic kitchen movement and his deli provides Noma-style food with a focus on baked products.

9 Dora
MAP C5 ▪ Værnedamsvej 6 ▪ 93 92 72 20 ▪ www.shopdora.dk

Stylish and playful homewares, beautiful jewellery, fun stationery and more; all with reasonable price tags.

10 DANSK Made for Rooms
MAP C5 ▪ Istedgade 80 ▪ 32 18 02 55 ▪ www.danskmadeforrooms.dk

An enclave of slick Danish design, from kitchen appliances to decor. Great for window-shopping on Vesterbo's vibrant high street.

Places to Eat

PRICE CATEGORIES

For a three-course meal for one without alcohol, including taxes and charges.
....
Ⓚ under 300 Dkr Ⓚ Ⓚ 300–500 Dkr
Ⓚ Ⓚ Ⓚ over 500 Dkr

1 Gorilla

MAP D6 ■ Flæsketorvet 63 ■ 33 33 83 30 ■ Opening hours vary, check website ■ www.restaurantgorilla.dk ■ Ⓚ Ⓚ

Tuck into shared plates of organic, sumptuous Scandi-tapas while slurping biodynamic wines at this trendy brasserie-style restaurant set in Kødbyen.

2 DØP

MAP J4

■ Købmagergade 52 ■ 30 20 40 25 ■ Open 10:30am–6:30pm Mon–Sat, 11am–6pm Sun ■ Ⓚ

This popular restaurant is known for some of the city's best organic hot dogs.

3 Tommi's Burger Joint

MAP B3 ■ Høkerboderne 21–23, Kødbyen ■ 33 31 00 11 ■ Open 11am–9pm Sun–Thu (until 10pm Fri & Sat) ■ Ⓚ

Cosy and child-friendly, this pint-size burger bar is in the heart of Copenhagen's meatpacking district.

4 Cofoco

MAP C5 ■ Abel Cathrines Gade 7 ■ 33 13 60 60 ■ www.cofoco.dk ■ Ⓚ

Delicious and reasonably priced Mediterranean-Danish food is served at a communal table. Book ahead.

5 Café Bang & Jensen

MAP C6 ■ Istedgade 130 ■ 33 25 53 18 ■ www.bangogjensen.dk ■ Ⓚ

This former pharmacy is now a café and bar offering fun cocktails.

6 Famo

MAP C5 ■ Saxogade 3 ■ 33 23 22 50 ■ www.famo.dk ■ Ⓚ Ⓚ

Locals head here for good-quality, inexpensive Italian cuisine.

7 Frederiks Have

MAP A4 ■ Smallegade 41 ■ 38 88 33 35 ■ Open noon–midnight Mon–Sat (until 5pm Sun) ■ www.frederikshave.dk ■ Ⓚ Ⓚ

Housed in a 19th-century building, Frederiks Have serves Swedish and Danish specialities.

8 Mother

MAP C6

■ Høkerboderne 9–15 ■ 22 27 58 98 ■ www.mother.dk ■ Ⓚ

A pizzeria known for organic sourdough bases, Mother has a variety of toppings.

Pizza with tomato topping, Mother

9 Formel B

MAP B5

■ Vesterbrogade 182 ■ 33 25 10 66 ■ Closed Sun ■ www.formelb.dk ■ Ⓚ Ⓚ Ⓚ

Enjoy delicate small plates made with farm-fresh ingredients here (see p60).

10 Les Trois Cochons

MAP C5 ■ Værnedamsvej 10 ■ 33 31 70 55 ■ Ⓚ Ⓚ

Aptly named ("the three pigs" in French), this restaurant serves great southern French food, all day long.

Dining booths at Les Trois Cochons

See map on pp86–7

🔟 Christianshavn and Holmen

After the Inner City, this settlement on the island of Amager is the oldest part of Copenhagen. In 1521, Christian II invited Dutch gardeners (whom he held in high regard) to this fertile area to plant and run market gardens. A century later, Christian IV built fortifications in the area and a town on an island at the north end. The canals of Christianshavn, lined with houseboats and pretty 17th-century houses, are a charming attraction. Holmen to the north consists of three artificial islets and was created in 1690 as a naval base. After the navy left in the late 20th century, the area saw an increase in public spaces, housing and art and design schools; it is also home to the city's impressive Opera House.

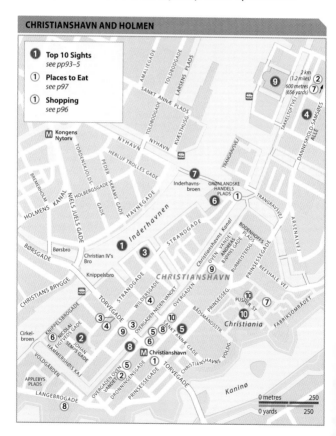

CHRISTIANSHAVN AND HOLMEN

① Top 10 Sights
see pp93–5

① Places to Eat
see p97

① Shopping
see p96

1 Inderhavnen
MAP J6–M4

Christianshavn is dominated by waterways. Its canals are tributaries of the Inner Harbour (Inderhavnen), which separates it from the rest of the city, eventually widening to become the Øresund (Sound). A harbour tour is a great way to appreciate the area.

2 Christians Kirke
MAP K6 ▪ Strandgade 1 ▪ 32 54 15 76 ▪ Open 10am–4pm Tue–Fri ▪ www.christianskirke.com

Originally known as Frederiks Kirke, this yellow-brick church was renamed Christians Kirke (after Christian IV, founder of this part of Copenhagen) in 1901. It was built between 1755 and 1759 in the Rococo style by Nicolai Eigtved, Frederik V's master architect. The interior resembles a theatre, with second-level seating galleries and the altar taking the place of the stage. The elegant tower was added by Eigtved's son-in-law, G D Anthon, 10 years after the church was built.

3 Harbour Circle
MAP K6–L5

Completed in 2017, the Harbour Circle route is part of Copenhagen's push for sustainable urban transport. The scenic pedestrian and cyclist path connects previously disjointed neighbourhoods along the city harbour, from Holmen and Nyhavn in the north to Christianshavn and southernmost Slusen. The route is connected by architecturally noteworthy bridges. Inderhavnsbroen

Inderhavnsbroen bridge

(built 2016), nicknamed "The Kissing Bridge", connects Nyhavn and the city centre with Christianshavn and Holmen. Platforms on the bridge offer spectacular views of the harbour area. Danish-Icelandic architect Olafur Eliasson designed the striking Cirkelbroen (The Circle Bridge): five touching circular platforms with ship masts link central Christianshavn to Appelbys Plads.

4 Gammel Dok
MAP L5 ▪ National Workshops for Art, Strandgade 27B ▪ 32 96 05 10

Gammel Dok ("Old Dock") was built in 1739, a time when the navy's ships moored in the local area. Denmark's first dry dock, it was located at this site till 1919. The warehouse dates back to 1882 and the building was acquired by the Danish state in 1979, when it was restored. It now serves as a popular historical site, and is also home to the National Workshops for Art. Artists, designers and restorers can apply for a residency to practise their craft here.

Gammel Dok on the waterfront

⑤ Holmen and Refshaleøen
MAP M4

North of Christianshavn are Holmen and Refshaleøen, a former shipyard that is home to various sporting activities and is now a major dining destination. Here you'll find innovative restaurants, stylish bakeries and the organic street food market, Reffen (see p97).

North Atlantic House, a former warehouse

⑥ Vor Frelsers Kirke
MAP L6 ▪ Sankt Annae Gade 29 ▪ 32 54 68 83 ▪ Church and Tower: open 9am–8pm daily ▪ Adm for tower, free with Copenhagen Card & City Pass ▪ www.vorfrelserskirke.dk

This magnificent Baroque church was built in 1682–96 by the Dutch-Norwegian architect Lambert van Haven in the form of a Greek cross. Its trademark twisted tower was added 50 years later. Inside the church, keep an eye out for the putti-covered font, presented in 1702 by Frederik IV's wife, Anna Sophie. The altarpiece is a must-see – it represents God as the Sun and depicts the scene in the garden of Gethsemane.

⑦ North Atlantic House
MAP M4 ▪ Strandgade 91 ▪ 32 83 37 00 ▪ Open 10am–5pm Mon–Fri, noon–5pm Sat & Sun ▪ Adm, under-12s free ▪ www.nordatlantens.dk

The North Atlantic House is a cultural centre for Greenland, Iceland and the Faroes. It is housed in an 18th-century warehouse, formerly the Greenlandic Trading Square, which hosts art displays and events.

⑧ Overgaden Neden Vandet and Overgaden Oven Vandet
MAP L6–M5

These two cobbled streets lie on either side of the Christianshavns canal. Overgaden Neden Vandet ("upper street below the water") is the quayside that runs along the Sound side of the canal. It is lined with 17th-century buildings. Overgaden Oven Vandet ("upper street above the water") is also lined with 17th-century houses.

⑨ Operaen
MAP M3 ▪ Ekvipagemestervej 10 ▪ 33 69 69 69 ▪ Guided tours available ▪ www.kglteater.dk

Completed in 2004, the Opera House was the first major public building to be built in the Holmen area after the navy vacated the docks. Architect Henning Larsen emphasized its location near the water, creating a building with large glass windows and

The twisted tower of Vor Frelsers Kirke

no pillars on the ground floor so as not to obstruct the view. The interior was designed to have a maritime feel as well, with big balconies, open spaces and white railings. The position of the Opera House caused major controversy when it was built, as it lies directly opposite Amalienborg. The design of the Opera House was also the cause of some friction when its benefactor, Mærsk McKinney Møller, insisted that his own ideas be incorporated into the construction. It is among the most expensive opera houses ever built, owing to its marble foyer and gold-leaf auditorium ceiling.

Modern interior of Operaen

10 Christiania
MAP M5

This rebellious squatters' enclave *(see pp28–9)*, set up in the 1970s in abandoned military barracks, was an inspirational new society with its own set of laws, readily available drugs and no tax system. The area has now become a bit more conventional; the inhabitants have been paying taxes since 1994. In 2011, residents and the state came to an agreement giving Christiania residents the right to buy, making the squat official for the first time. There are no sights per se but many hippy hangouts.

A WALKING TOUR OF THE AREA

▶ MORNING

Start at the Knippelsbro bridge. Built in 1937, the bridge takes its name from Hans Knip, the tollkeeper. Turn right to visit **Christians Kirke** *(see p41)* on Strandgade. Head north on Johan Semps Gade to catch a glimpse of **Den Sorte Diamant** library *(see p12)* across the harbour, then head west to cross **Cirkelbroen** *(see p93)*, a pedestrian and bike bridge. Follow the path past Appelbys Plads to **Overgaden Oven Vandet**. Take a left and walk along the canal. Stop at No. 32 (built in 1622–4), on Strandgade, which is said to be the oldest house in Christianshavn. From here, turn right onto Sankt Annæ Gade to see **Vor Frelsers Kirke**. If you are curious about **Christiania**, follow Overgaden Oven Vandet until you can take a right down Brobergsgade, passing through the gate reading "You are now leaving the EU". Alternatively, stroll canalside and go right at Bodenhoffs Plads, then head left onto Værftsbroen. Keep walking towards the **Operaen**. Hop on a harbour bus back to Knippelsbro for lunch at **Café Wilder** *(see p97)* on Wildersgade.

AFTERNOON

Spend the afternoon shopping. If you are in the mood for a drink, there are many cafés all along the Christianshavns Kanal. Linger over supper at **Restaurant Barr** *(Strandgade; 32 96 32 93)* or catch a performance at the **Opera House** (taking bus No. 9A or the harbour bus from Knippelsbro).

See map on p92 ←

Shopping

1 Bit Antik

MAP L6 ▪ Prinsessegade 17B
▪ 40 72 09 62 ▪ Open 3–6pm Wed

This tiny shop is filled with pieces from Denmark's yesteryears, including old dolls and doll houses, books, glasses, sculpture as well as porcelain objects.

2 Aurum
MAP L6
▪ Dronningensgade 23
▪ 25 30 00 11 ▪ www.
aurumcph.com

Some 20 international jewellers, including Marco Vallejo, are represented at Aurum. Many materials, such as precious stones, are used to create these unique pieces.

Gold ring by Marco Vallejo

3 Porte à Gauche
MAP L5 ▪ Torvegade 20 ▪ 32 54 01 40 ▪ www.porteagauche.dk

A trendy boutique that offers chic, minimalist Scandinavian designer wear for women, here you will find a classic, elegant collection of Julie Sandlau jewellery.

4 Mo Christianshavn
MAP L5 ▪ Torvegade 24
▪ 26 80 17 26 ▪ Open by appointment only ▪ www.mo.dk

A small shop and workshop of a popular local jewellery designer.

5 Ganni Postmodern
MAP L6 ▪ Overgaden Oven Vandet 40 ▪ 28 35 55 56 ▪ www.ganni.com

This is the first Ganni Postmodern concept store in the city. The Ganni headquarters are also in Copenhagen, and there are stores across the world.

6 Lagkagehuset
MAP L6 ▪ Torvegade 45
▪ 32 57 36 07 ▪ Open from 6am daily

Well known for its breads, cakes and pastries, this bakery has a fine selection during Christmas.

7 Kvindesmedien
MAP M5 ▪ Mælkevejen 83 ▪ 32 57 76 58 ▪ www.kvindesmedien.dk

An artistic workshop that offers high quality steel design, this is the place. for one of a kind decorations and sculptures.

8 Hilbert København
MAP L6 ▪ Sankt Annæ Gade 24 ▪ 33 93 53 01 ▪ www.hilbertkbh.com

Jewellery is made to order here by goldsmith Morten Hilbert.

9 Cibi e Vini
MAP L5 ▪ Torvegade 28
▪ 32 57 77 98 ▪ www.cibievini.dk

At this Italian delicatessen, enjoy wine, bread, pasta and meats.

10 Bevar Christiania Boden
MAP M5 ▪ Sydområdet 32 A

Located close to Pusher Street, Bevar Christiania Boden sells a wide range of charming Christiania souvenirs to take back home.

Souvenirs outside Christiania Shop

Places to Eat

PRICE CATEGORIES
For a three-course meal for one without alcohol, including taxes and charges.
....
⊛ under 300 Dkr ⊛⊛ 300–500 Dkr
⊛⊛⊛ over 500 Dkr

1 **POPL Burger**
MAP M4 ▪ Strandgade 108
▪ 32 96 32 92 ▪ ⊛

A Noma offshoot that serves simple, organic burgers (beef, vegetarian or vegan) using finely crafted ingredients from Noma's own fermentation lab.

2 **Reffen**
MAP B2 ▪ Refshalevej 167 Unit A ▪ 33 93 07 60 ▪ Opening hours vary, check website ▪ www.reffen.dk ▪ ⊛

The city's street food hub offers a taste of international and local cuisines from around the world in casual, grungy surroundings.

3 **Blue House Sandwich**
MAP L6 ▪ Torvegade 34 C
▪ 32 95 17 15 ▪ www.bluehouse. dk ▪ ⊛

A popular sandwich bar that draws a mixed crowd for its baguette-style sandwiches, packed to the brim with savoury ingredients.

4 **Café Wilder**
MAP L5 ▪ Wildersgade 56
▪ 32 54 71 83 ▪ www.cafewilder.dk
▪ ⊛⊛

French and Danish dishes, accompanied by wine and local beer, are the specialities at this small, cosy café. Hot drinks are also available.

5 **Sofiekælderen**
MAP L6 ▪ Overgaden Oven Vandet 32 ▪ 32 57 77 01 ▪ Closed Sun & Mon ▪ www.sofiekaelderen.dk ▪ ⊛⊛

Close to the water, this café-bar turns into a nightclub on weekends with DJ playing music.

6 **No. 2**
MAP K6 ▪ Nicolai Eigtveds Gade 32 ▪ 33 11 11 68 ▪ ⊛ ⊛

A fine dining establishment, restaurant No. 2 offers a good selection of wine, hearty meals and peerless sea views.

Chic interiors of Noma

7 **Noma**
MAP B2 ▪ Refshalevej 96
▪ 32 96 32 97 ▪ Closed Sun–Tue
▪ www.noma.dk ▪ ⊛ ⊛ ⊛

Copenhagen's ultimate Michelin-star restaurant, Noma *(see p61)*, specializes in New Nordic cuisine. It's due to close its doors at the end of 2024, so expect demand for bookings to be high.

8 **Rabes Have**
MAP K6 ▪ Langebrogade 8
▪ 32 57 34 17 ▪ Open 11am–4pm Wed–Sun ▪ ⊛

Opened for soldiers and sailors in 1632, this is the oldest pub in the city.

9 **Parterre**
MAP M5 ▪ Overgaden Oven Vandet 90 ▪ ⊛

A gorgeous basement café on Christianshavn's canal. It is excellent for breakfast and lunch.

10 **Oven Vande Café**
MAP L5 ▪ Overgaden Oven Vandet 44 ▪ 32 95 96 02 ▪ www. cafeovenvande.dk ▪ ⊛ ⊛

Order a tasty salad, soup or panini at this café with outdoor seating.

See map on p92

🔟 Beyond Copenhagen

Although Copenhagen itself can entertain you for days, the area around the city also offers many excursion options. Roskilde and Helsingør provide a taste of Nordic history, up to the founding of Copenhagen. Get a sense of medieval maritime defence of the Sound at Helsingør's Kronborg Slot or explore royal lifestyles of the 17th and 18th centuries at Frederiksborg and Charlottenlund. Art- and literature-lovers will enjoy Arken, Louisiana, Ordrupgaard and the Karen Blixen Museet. Frilandsmuseet and Den Blå Planet, National Aquarium Denmark are must-visits for kids.

Windmill at Frilandsmuseet

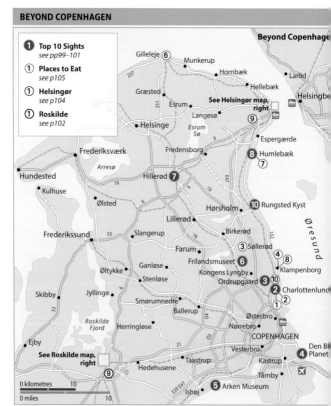

BEYOND COPENHAGEN

❶	Top 10 Sights see pp99–101
①	Places to Eat see p105
①	Helsingør see p104
①	Roskilde see p102

Replica Viking longboats on the water in Roskilde

1 Roskilde

The town of Roskilde makes for a fascinating day out. You will find a medieval cathedral, a royal burial site and the wonderful Viking Ship Museum *(see p102)*, which offers fjord trips on replica Viking longboats.

2 Charlottenlund Slotshave

MAP B2 ■ Open daily ■ www. kongeligeslotte.dk

The park around Charlottenlund Slot is a 16-minute train ride from the city centre. Redesigned in the Romantic English style in the 19th century, the park includes a charming thatched cottage, once lodgings for the Royal Life Guards. The palace itself is closed to the public.

3 Ordrupgaard

MAP B2 ■ Vilvordevej 110, Charlottenlund ■ 39 64 11 83 ■ Gallery: open 1–5pm Tue, Thu & Fri, 11am–9pm Wed (until 5pm Sat & Sun); Finn Juhl's House: open 11am–5pm Sat & Sun ■ Adm, under-18s free ■ Book ahead for guided tours in English; free audio guide ■ www. ordrupgaard.dk

This gallery has a collection of French Impressionist art and works by 19th- and 20th-century Danish artists. The 19th-century mansion has an extension by the late architect Zaha Hadid and a gallery dedicated to furniture designer Finn Juhl's work.

The interior of Finn Juhl's house

Marine life at Den Blå Planet

4 Den Blå Planet, National Aquarium Denmark

MAP C3 ■ Jacob Fortlingsvej 1, Kastrup ■ 44 22 22 44 ■ Open 10am–5pm daily (until 9pm Mon) ■ Adm, free with Copenhagen Card & City Pass ■ www.denblaaplanet.dk

Denmark's national aquarium Den Blå Planet is famous for its architecture inspired by the currents of a whirlpool (the lobby is akin to a vortex). With 53 aquariums and installations, it is said to be the most modern aquarium in Northern Europe.

5 Arken Museum for Moderne Kunst

MAP B3 ■ Skovvej 100, Ishøj ■ 43 54 02 22 ■ Open 10am–5pm Tue–Sun (until 9pm Wed) ■ Adm, free with Copenhagen Card ■ www.arken.dk

This wonderful museum houses a rotating permanent collection of contemporary international and Danish art, along with temporary exhibitions. The white, ship-like museum building, designed by Danish architect Søren Lund, could be an exhibit in itself. It offers great views of the sea at Køge Bugt.

6 Frilandsmuseet

MAP B2 ■ Konggevejen 100, Kongens Lyngby ■ 41 20 64 55 ■ Opening hours vary, check website ■ Adm ■ en.natmus.dk

Part of the Nationalmuseet (see pp32–3), Denmark's Open Air Museum has working exhibits from the period 1650–1940. Explore farms, windmills and a cooperative village. There are old Danish breeds of livestock, including pigs, sheep and geese.

7 Frederiksborg Slot

MAP B2 ■ DK-3400 Hillerød ■ 48 26 04 39 ■ Museum: open Apr–Oct: 10am–5pm daily, Nov–Mar: 11am–3pm daily; Baroque gardens: open 10am–sunset daily ■ Adm (museum only) ■ www.dnm.dk

This copper-turreted castle (see p42) is situated on three islets in a lake that is surrounded by Baroque gardens. It was built in 1602–20 for Christian IV. The interior is a mix of Renaissance and Baroque decor. After a fire in 1859, the castle was rescued from ruin by J C Jacobsen (of Carlsberg fame), who founded a museum here.

The Great Hall at Frederiksborg Slot

8 Louisiana Museum

MAP B1 ■ Gammel Strandvej 13, Humlebæk ■ 49 19 07 19 ■ Open 11am–10pm Tue–Fri, 11am–6pm Sat & Sun ■ Adm, under-18s free ■ Guided tours available in English ■ www.louisiana.dk

This museum *(see p103)* houses an impressive selection of works by international artists like Picasso and Francis Bacon, and Danish masters including Asger Jorn and Per Kirkeby. There is also a children's wing, which offers art-related activities for kids aged between 3 and 16 years. The coastal location, sculpture park and excellent café make the museum even more appealing for visitors.

Courtyard at Kronborg Slot

9 Helsingør

In the 1400s, this harbour town *(see p104)* levied tax on all sea traffic that passed through the Sound. A pretty medieval centre aside, there is the 16th-century castle, Kronborg Slot, the Carmelite monastery and the Maritime Museum of Denmark.

10 Karen Blixen Museet

MAP B2 ■ Rungsted Strandvej 111, Rungsted Kyst ■ 45 57 10 57 ■ Open 11am–8pm Tue–Fri (until 5pm Sat & Sun) ■ Adm, under-18s free ■ Book ahead for guided tours in English ■ www.blixen.dk

Karen Blixen (pen name: Isak Dinesen), the author of the acclaimed memoir *Out of Africa*, was born here in 1885. When she was 28, Blixen left for Kenya with her husband to establish a coffee plantation. She returned in 1931 and the house is exactly as it was when she used to live here.

DAY TOUR BEYOND COPENHAGEN

▶ MORNING

From Københavns Hovedbanegård (Copenhagen Central Station), take a train and head to the town of **Helsingør** to explore the local museums and castles. Have a wander around **Kronborg Slot** *(see p104)*, a lovely 16th-century castle with a banqueting hall, royal chambers and casemates, and see why it was immortalized as Elsinore in Hamlet. After your castle tour, stop by the **Maritime Museum of Denmark** *(see p104)*. For lunch, return to the town square and sit down for an open sandwich and a beer at one of its numerous pubs. After lunch, wander through the medieval streets, especially Stendgade and Strandgade *(see p104)*. Visit the medieval **Domkirke** and the **Bymuseum** *(see p104)*, housed in a small Carmelite hospital dating back to 1520.

AFTERNOON

Take the train to Humlebæk and visit the **Louisiana Museum**, *(Strandvej 13, Humlebaek Gl)* which stays open until 10pm on Tuesdays to Fridays. You can book a guided tour that covers the museum's *(see p103)* architecture and landscape. Then return to the station and take a train to Rungsted Kyst and drop in at the Karen Blixen Museet. After a walk around the house, garden and bird sanctuary, have coffee and one of the homemade cakes at the museum café. Head back towards Copenhagen in the early evening, stopping off en route at Klampenborg for dinner and an evening of entertainment at the **Bakken** *(see p52)* funfair.

See map on p98 ⟵

Roskilde

1 Roskilde Domkirke
MAP P6 ■ Domkirkestræde 3
■ 46 35 16 24 ■ Opening hours vary
■ Adm, free with Copenhagen City
Pass ■ www.roskildedomkirke.dk
This UNESCO World Heritage Site
houses the mortal remains of
40 Danish monarchs.

Replica Viking vessels

2 Vikingeskibsmuseet
MAP P4 ■ Vindeboder 12 ■ 46
30 02 00 ■ Open 10am–5pm daily
■ Adm, under-18s free ■ www.viking
eskibsmuseet.dk
The Viking Ship Museum displays five
1,000-year-old Viking vessels. Boat
trips available from May to September.

3 Roskilde Museum
MAP P5 ■ Sankt Ols Stræde
3 ■ 46 31 65 00 ■ Open 10am–
4pm Tue–Sun ■ Adm, free with
Copenhagen City Pass ■ www.
roskildemuseum.dk
This museum illustrates Roskilde's
history from the time when it was
Denmark's first capital.

4 Roskilde Kloster
MAP P6 ■ Sankt Peders Straede
8E ■ 46 35 02 19 ■ www.roskilde
kloster.dk
A former convent, this was Denmark's
first refuge for unmarried mothers.

5 Skomagergade and Algade
MAP P6
The city's two main cobbled streets
are lined with shops and cafés.

6 Hestetorvet
MAP Q6
The Horse Market Place is set in
what was Roskilde's largest square
for centuries. Three giant vases here
were created by artist Peter Brandes.

7 Kirkegård
MAP Q6
Now a park, this former medieval
churchyard holds the graves of many
prominent Roskilde citizens.

8 Stændertorvet
MAP P6 ■ Markets: open
Wed & Sat
The city's central square in front of
the Town Hall has been a market-
place since the Middle Ages.

9 RAGNAROCK
Rabalderstræde 16 ■ 46 31
68 54 ■ Open 10am–5pm daily
■ Adm ■ www.museumragnarock.dk
Founded in 2016, this museum
dedicated to pop, rock and youth
culture offers a kaleidoscopic
journey that aims to engage,
educate, and inspire visitors.

10 Roskilde Palace
MAP P6 ■ Stændertorvet 3D
■ 33 95 42 00 ■ Open 9am–6pm daily
(summer: until 8pm) ■ www.slks.dk/
omraader/slotte-og-ejendomme/
slotte-og-haver/roskilde-palae
Built in 1733–6 for royal visitors, the
Roskilde Palace is a striking yellow,
four-wing Baroque building. The
grounds are often used for exhibitions,
concerts and other cultural events.

The vibrant Roskilde Palace

Louisiana Museum

Visitors outside the old villa at Louisiana Museum

 Big Thumb (1968)
Modelled after the thumb of its creator, French sculptor César Baldaccini (1921–98), this striking, sculpture is 2 m (6 ft) tall.

 Dead Drunk Danes (1960)
Rebel artist Asger Jorn (1914–73) was awarded the Guggenheim International Award for this abstract painting in 1964. However, he rejected it and sent Harry Guggenheim a telegram: "Go to hell with your money bastard *stop* Never asked for it *stop* Against all decency to mix artist against his will in your publicity *stop*".

 3 Gleaming Lights of the Souls (2008)
Japanese artist Yayoi Kusama's lyrical installation has mirrors and 100 lamps resembling glowing ping pong balls.

 House to Watch the Sunset (2015)
Swiss artist Not Vital's house of steel blends in with its surroundings as it reflects the nature and changing seasons of the Sculpture Park in its shiny surface.

 Little Janey Waney (1964/76)
This mobile installation by American artist Alexander Calder is a colourful sight, moving elegantly whenever the wind blows.

 Alberto Giacometti Collection
The museum owns an impressive collection of 13 sculptures and several drawings by Giacometti (1901–66). The elongated figures with rough textures are reminiscent of African sculpture.

Two Piece Reclining Figure No 5 (1963–4)
A bronze work by Henry Moore (1898–1986), this exhibit occupies a beautiful spot between the trees, its humanoid, organic forms melding with the landscape.

The Louisiana Butik
The museum shop carries a variety of high-quality Scandinavian design products, art and culture books and exhibition posters.

The Louisiana Cafe
One of Denmark's most beautiful panoramic views over the Øresund to the coast of Sweden can be experienced here. The kitchen serves contemporary Danish cuisine made with fresh seasonal produce.

The Sculpture Park
In the museum's sculpture park dotted by around 60 sculptures, the visual arts, architecture and landscapes exist in unity. The views are as much a part of the park's charm as its exhibits.

See map on p98

Helsingør

1 Maritime Museum of Denmark

MAP Q2 ▪ Ny Kronborgvej 1 ▪ 49 21 06 85 ▪ Open Jan–Jun & Sep–Dec: 11am–5pm Tue–Sun; Jul–Aug: 11am–6pm daily ▪ Adm, free with Copenhagen City Pass, under-18s free ▪ www.mfs.dk

This interactive museum features hands-on digital exhibits.

2 Festivals

www.visitnordsjaelland.com

Helsingør's summer festivals include the CLICK festival (May), PASSAGE street theater festival (late July to early August) and the Shakespeare festival (August).

3 Karmeliterklosteret

MAP P2 ▪ Sankt Anna Gade 38 ▪ 49 21 17 74 ▪ Open May–mid-Sep: 10am–3pm Tue, mid-Sep–Apr: 10am–2pm Tue–Sun ▪ Adm ▪ www.sctmariae.dk

The Carmelite Order owned this 15th-century Gothic-style monastery.

4 Helsingør Bymuseum

MAP P2 ▪ Sankt Anna Gade 36 ▪ 49 28 18 00 ▪ Opening hours vary, check website ▪ Adm ▪ www.helsingormuseer.dk/bymuseet

Once a sailors' hospital, its exhibits recall its history and that of this medieval town.

5 Kronborg Slot

MAP Q2 ▪ Kronborg 2C ▪ 49 21 30 78 ▪ Open Jan–Apr, Nov & Dec: 11am–4pm Tue–Sun; May–Oct: 10am–5pm daily ▪ Adm, free with Copenhagen Card ▪ www.kongeligeslotte.dk

Said to be the setting of Shakespeare's *Hamlet*, this castle (*see p42*) was built in 1420.

6 Culture Yard

MAP P3 ▪ Havnepladsen 1 ▪ 49 28 37 70 ▪ Open 8am–7pm Mon, Wed & Fri (until 4pm Tue, Sat & Sun, until 8pm Thu) ▪ www.kuto.dk

With a multimedia library, cultural activities, and a café, this is a cultural house overlooking Kronborg Slot.

7 Stengade and Strandgade

MAP P3 ▪ www.helsingormuseer.dk

Stengade is a pedestrianized street in the medieval quarter. Some houses on the parallel Strandgade date back to the 1400s.

8 Sankt Olai Kirke (Helsingør Domkirke)

MAP P2 ▪ Sankt Anna Gade 12 ▪ 49 21 04 43 ▪ Open May–Aug: 10am–4pm daily; Sep–Apr: 10am–2pm daily ▪ www.helsingoerdomkirke.dk

Note the 15th-century crucifix, 1568 Renaissance pulpit, 1579 baptismal font and carved wooden altar.

9 Danmarks Teknisk Museum

Fabriksvej 25 ▪ 49 22 26 11 ▪ Open Feb–Oct: 10am–5pm Tue–Sun (Nov–Jan: until 4pm) ▪ Adm, under-18s free ▪ www.tekniskmuseum.dk

The machines at this museum of science and technology include steam engines, cars and aeroplanes.

10 Øresundsakvariet

MAP P1 ▪ Strandpromenaden 5 ▪ 35 32 19 70 ▪ Open Jun–Aug: 10am–6pm daily; Sep–May: 10am–4pm daily (until 5pm Sat & Sun) ▪ Adm ▪ www.oresundsakvariet.ku.dk

This small aquarium has a variety of tropical fish and Baltic species.

A yacht sailing past Kronborg Slot

Places to Eat

1 Café Bomhuset

MAP B2 ▪ Skovriderkroen, Strandvejen 235, Charlottenlund ▪ 39 65 67 00 ▪ www.cafebomhuset. dk ▪ ⓀⓀ

An upscale alternative to the typical outdoor café. The terrace is popular.

2 Café Jorden Rundt

MAP B2 ▪ Strandvejen 152, Charlottenlund ▪ 39 63 73 81 ▪ Ⓚ

Popular for brunch, sandwiches and cakes, this café also offers great sea views from its panoramic windows.

3 Søllerød Kro

MAP B2

▪ Søllerødvej 35, Holte ▪ 45 80 25 05 ▪ Opening hours vary; check website ▪ www. soelleroed-kro.dk ▪ ⓀⓀⓀ

This Michelin-starred restaurant has set menus and à la carte dishes.

4 Den Gule Cottage

MAP B2 ▪ Taarbæk Strandvej 2, Klampenborg ▪ 39 64 06 91 ▪ Open noon–9pm Tue–Sun ▪ www.dengule cottage.dk ▪ ⓀⓀ

This cottage was designed in 1844 by the great Danish architect Gottlieb Bindesbøll. Dishes are prepared with seasonal ingredients.

5 Mumm

MAP N6 ▪ Karen Olsdatters Stræde 9, Roskilde ▪ 46 37 22 01 ▪ Open 5:30pm–midnight Tue–Sat ▪ ⓀⓀⓀ

On one of Roskilde's oldest streets, this upscale, tiny French-Danish restaurant has a pretty courtyard.

6 Restaurant Gilleleje Havn

MAP A1 ▪ Havnevej 14, Gilleleje ▪ Opening hours vary, check website ▪ www.gillelejehavn.dk ▪ ⓀⓀ

Enjoy traditional Danish seafood at this 19th-century seamen's inn.

7 Restaurant Sletten

MAP B2 ▪ Gl. Strandvej 137, Humlebæk ▪ 49 19 13 21 ▪ Open noon–3pm & 6–11pm Tue–Sun (until midnight Fri–Sat) ▪ ⓀⓀⓀ

Sletten serves excellent value French cuisine, with the bonus of a sea view.

The stylish interior of Den Røde Cottage

8 Den Røde Cottage

MAP B2 ▪ Strandvejen 550, Klampenborg ▪ 31 90 46 14 ▪ Open 6pm–midnight Wed–Sat ▪ www. denroedecottage.dk ▪ ⓀⓀ

The sophisticated sister to Den Gule Cottage next door, Den Røde offers exquisite seasonal menus.

9 Snekken

MAP P4 ▪ Vindeboder 16, Roskilde ▪ 46 35 98 16 ▪ www. snekken.dk ▪ ⓀⓀ

Locals book a table at Snekken for contemporary cuisine and sea views.

10 MASH Skovriderkroen

MAP B2 ▪ Strandvejen 235, Charlottenlund ▪ 33 13 93 00 ▪ Closed Sat & Sun L ▪ www.mash steak.dk ▪ ⓀⓀ

World-famous American steakhouse with a great wine list to match.

See map on p98–9

Streetsmart

Bicycles lined up outside a timber
framed building in the old town

Getting Around

Arriving by Air

Airlines flying directly to **Copenhagen Airport** include **Scandinavian Airlines**, **British Airways**, **easyJet** and **Norwegian**. The airport is located in Kastrup, 12 km (7 miles) southeast of the city. It takes around 15 minutes to reach the city centre by train or Metro (the station is near Terminal 3), or 45 minutes by bus (both cost the same). There is also a taxi rank just outside Terminal 3. Expect to pay around 300 Dkr for a cab to the city centre.

Arriving by Train

Copenhagen is connected by train to many European cities, including Hamburg, Berlin and Stockholm. All international trains stop at the large Københavns Hovedbanegård central station, part of **Danish State Railways** (DSB). If you plan to travel on to Sweden, remember to bring your passport with you as there could be a border check at the first train stop in Sweden.

Arriving by Road

There are two main international road routes into Copenhagen. The first is from Sweden, via the **Øresund Bridge** from Malmö. The other option is to drive from Germany via the Danish island of Funen, from where you can cross the **Great Belt Bridge** to Sjælland, the island on which the city of Copenhagen lies. Both bridges exact a toll.

Arriving by Ferry

Ferries to Copenhagen leave from Swinoujscie in Poland (operated by **Polferries**), and Oslo in Norway (run by **DFDS Seaways**). There are no direct ferry routes between the UK and Denmark.

Public Transport

Arriva buses, DSB local trains and **Metro Service** rapid transit systems are fast and reliable, with certain routes running 24/7. You can take a bike for free onto S-trains (S-tog), but there are generally peak-hour restrictions on the Metro.

In Greater Copenhagen, you can use a single ticket or buy a **Rejsekort**, a prepaid smart card that can be topped up and used on all three systems. Smart cards work out cheaper than individual tickets, but you can only purchase them from stations. Most S-tog stations have a 7/11 convenience store doubling as a ticket office. DOT Mobilbilletter, an app developed by **DOT**, can be used to buy passes for all modes of transportation. Tickets must always be validated before travel; there are severe fines for travelling without one. Be careful when entering and exiting the bus, as you may cross a bike lane and bikes have the right of way.

Harbour Bus

Harbour buses (991, 992, 993) run the length of the city's harbour between Nordre Toldbod (near the Gefionspringvandet fountain), past Den Sorte Diamant to Teglholmen, south of Fisketorvet. Times vary, but they run roughly every 15 minutes during peak times and hourly otherwise. Harbour buses use the same ticket or card as other modes of transport.

Taxi and Rickshaw

Available taxis have a "fri" (free) sign on the roof, but hailing one can prove a challenge. It can often be quicker to find a taxi rank; most S-train and Metro stations will have one nearby. The biggest firms in Denmark are **Taxa** and DanTaxi; both offer a credit card payment option and receipts. For an open-air ride, you can catch the cycle rickshaws for short rides from Storkespringvandet, Tivoli, Rådhuspladsen and Nyhavn, but beware – this method of transport can be rather expensive.

Driving

You can drive in Denmark if you are over 18 and hold a valid licence. Always carry the registration papers and a reflecting triangle – and always watch out for cyclists. There are several good car share schemes in operation around the city, the most popular being **Drive Now** and **LetsGo**, which offer a very good, cost-effective way of travelling long distances with larger groups. In Copenhagen, on-street parking in the city centre can be a challenge, and car parks are expensive. There are many parking apps, including **Easypark**, **Parkman** or **Parkpark**, which use your mobile phone's GPS to pinpoint your spot, and also enable you to pay online using a credit card. The street sign "Parkering forbudt" means no parking within certain time limits. Note that motoring offences attract on-the-spot fines.

Bus and Boat Tours

Enjoy the city at your own pace with the **Stromma** hop-on-hop-off bus tour, which covers all the city's top tourist hotspots. You can also explore Copenhagen's charming canals by boat. Tours depart from Nyhavn and Holmens Kanal, and you can choose either an hour-long grand tour or a hop-on-hop-off flexible day pass. Stromma, in Nyhavn, offers the biggest choice of tours, including some that have live music and on-board dining. **Netto Boats** (tours in English, German, Danish), also in Nyhavn, is a slightly cheaper but an equally good alternative.

Cycling

Denmark is a country of cyclists, with infrastructures supporting this green mode of transport. It's easy to join the locals in Copenhagen, which is home to more bikes than cars and has an unparalleled number of dedicated cycle paths. Although it is not mandatory to wear a helmet while cycling, it is certainly recommended. It is illegal to cycle at night without front and rear lights so make sure your rental bike is fitted with both; a bell can be handy, too. Comfortable electric bikes, with built-in GPS, can be used across the capital with the **Bycyklen** scheme. These are available year-round from stands across the city; you must register online to use them. You can find bikes via the **Donkey Republic** app. Stick to the cycle paths if available, and always stop to allow passengers onto and off buses.

Walking

Copenhagen is compact and flat, making it a joy to explore on foot. Many of the sights, especially those in the city centre, are just a short walk away from one other. Be sure that you do not confuse bike lanes with pedestrian pavements as this can be a painful mistake.

DIRECTORY

ARRIVING BY AIR

British Airways
w britishairways.com

Copenhagen Airport
w cph.dk/en

easyJet
w easyjet.com

Norwegian
w norwegian.com

Scandinavian Airlines
w sas.dk

ARRIVING BY TRAIN

Danish State Railways
w dsb.dk

ARRIVING BY ROAD

Great Belt Bridge
w storebaelt.dk

Øresund Bridge
w oresundsbron.com

ARRIVING BY FERRY

DFDS Seaways
w dfdsseaways.co.uk

Polferries
w polferries.com

PUBLIC TRANSPORT

Arriva
w arriva.dk

Metro Service
w m.dk

DOT
w dinoffentligetransport.dk

Rejsekort
w rejsekort.dk

TAXI AND RICKSHAW

DanTaxi
w dantaxi.dk

Taxa
w taxa.dk

DRIVING

DriveNow
w drive-now.com

Easypark
w easypark.dk

LetsGo
w letsgo.dk

Parkman
w parkman.dk

Parkpark
w parkpark.dk

BUS AND BOAT TOURS

Netto Boats
w havnerundfart.dk

Stromma
w stromma.dk

CYCLING

Bycyklen
w bycyklen.dk

Donkey Republic
w donkey.bike

Practical Information

Passports and Visas

For entry requirements, including visas, consult your nearest Danish embassy or check the **Danish Immigration Service** website. From late 2023, citizens of the UK, US, Canada, Australia and New Zealand do not need a visa for stays of up to three months, but must apply in advance for the European Travel Information and Authorization System (**ETIAS**). Visitors from other countries may also require an ETIAS, so check before travelling. EU nationals do not need a visa or an ETIAS.

Government Advice

Now more than ever, it is important to consult both your and the Danish government's advice before travelling. The **UK Foreign, Commonwealth & Development Office (FCDO)**, the **US Department of State**, the **Australian Department of Foreign Affairs and Trade** and the **Danish Ministry of Foreign Affairs** offer the latest information on security, health and local regulations.

Customs Information

You can find information on the laws relating to goods and currency taken in or out of Denmark on the **Danish Tax Agency** website. There are strict limits on what can be imported. Do not carry food items that have not been vacuum-packed by the manufacturer. Items in commercial quantities and gifts valued at more than 1,350 Dkr are also subject to customs duty. US citizens are liable to pay duty if carrying goods worth more than $400.

Insurance

We recommend taking out a comprehensive insurance policy covering theft, loss of belongings, medical care, cancellations and delays, and to read the small print carefully. Visitors are eligible for free emergency medical care in Denmark, provided they have a valid European Health Insurance Card (**EHIC**) or UK Global Health Insurance Card (**GHIC**). Medical cover is highly recommended, particularly for those without an EHIC or GHIC.

Health

Denmark's healthcare service is excellent. Emergency medical care in Denmark is free for all UK, EU and Australian citizens. If you have an EHIC or GHIC, be sure to present this as soon as possible. For other visitors, payment of medical expenses is the patient's responsibility. It is therefore important to arrange comprehensive medical insurance before travelling. **Rigshospitalet** is a good hospital for urgent care, while **Bispebjerg Hospital** has an A&E department. If you require emergency dental treatment, head to **Dentist Tandlægevagten**. Doctors' fee refunds can be obtained at the nearest municipal or health insurance office.

Pharmacists are readily available and can give advice and over-the-counter medication. Pharmacies, such as **Steno Apotek**, are generally open 24 hours a day; look for the *apotek* sign (denoted by a green "Å"). In an urgent situation that does not quite require an ambulance, call 1813 before going to an emergency room. This alerts an on-call physician or an appropriate hospital to your arrival. The 1813 service can also issue medical prescriptions, to be picked up at a nearby pharmacy.

Unless clearly stated otherwise, tap water in Copenhagen is safe to drink. For information regarding COVID-19 vaccination requirements, it is best to consult government advice.

Smoking, Alcohol and Drugs

Smoking is illegal at train stations and in indoor public spaces, with the exception of very small bars and pubs that do not serve food.

Denmark's blood alcohol limit for drivers is 0.05 per cent. Beer and wine can be bought in shops from 16 years of age and above, but in bars only from 18 years. Marijuana is illegal in Denmark though present in places such as Christiana, where police raids are routine.

ID

Passports may be requested when checking into a hotel and some form of photo ID may be requested at any time by police. It is advisable to carry a photocopy of your passport. Drivers must carry valid driving licences at all times.

Personal Security

On the whole, Copenhagen is a safe city to visit, where you only really need to fear becoming a victim of pickpocketing. Make sure your valuables are kept in a safe place, and be wary of pickpockets on public transport, particularly on crowded Metro trains. If you are a victim of a crime, contact the **Central Police Station** to file a report. You will be given a crime report note, which you will need for any insurance claims.

Copenhageners are generally very accepting of all people, regardless of their race, gender or sexuality. Homosexuality was legalized in 1933 and, in 1989, Denmark became the first country in the world to legally recognize same-sex partnerships. Copenhagen in particular prides itself on being an inclusive city, with a host of LGBTQ+-friendly bars and clubs, as well as annual community events. If you do feel unsafe, the **Safe Space Alliance** pinpoints your nearest place of refuge.

For ambulance or fire brigade, call **emergency** services.

Travellers With Specific Requirements

Most of Copenhagen is fairly accessible, although some shops and restaurants in the older parts of the city centre do not offer facilities for those with specific requirements. While the city is almost completely flat, its cobblestone roads can be a challenge for wheelchairs. All public transport is accessible. **DSB Handicap Service** has useful information on public transport accessibility, and the **Visit Copenhagen** office lists places that offer facilities for the travellers with specific requirements. **God Adgang** (Access Denmark) is also a great resource, listing and rating venues and service providers in Copenhagen and across Denmark more generally.

Time Zone

Copenhagen is on Central European Time (CET). Central European Summer Time (CEST) runs from the last Sunday in March to the last Sunday in October.

DIRECTORY

PASSPORTS AND VISAS

Danish Immigration Service
ⓦ nyidanmark.dk

ETIAS
ⓦ etiasvisa.com

GOVERNMENT ADVICE

Australian Department of Foreign Affairs and Trade
ⓦ smartraveller.gov.au

Danish Ministry of Foreign Affairs
ⓦ um.dk

UK Foreign, Commonwealth & Development Office (FCDO)
ⓦ gov.uk/foreign-travel-advice

US Department of State
ⓦ travel.state.gov

CUSTOMS INFORMATION

Danish Tax Agency
ⓦ skat.dk

INSURANCE

EHIC
ⓦ ec.europa.eu

GHIC
ⓦ gov.uk/global-healthinsurance-card

HEALTH

Bispebjerg Hospital
ⓦ bispebjerghospital.dk

Dentist Tandlægevagten
ⓦ dentalklinikken.dk

Rigshospitalet
ⓦ rigshospitalet.dk

Steno Apotek
ⓦ stenoapotek.dk

PERSONAL SECURITY

Central Police Station
ⓒ 33 14 88 88

Emergency
ⓒ 112/114

Safe Space Alliance
ⓦ safespacealliance.com

TRAVELLERS WITH SPECIFIC REQUIREMENTS

DSB Handicap Service
ⓒ 70 13 14 19

God Agang
ⓦ godadgang.dk

Visit Copenhagen
Vesterbrogade 4
ⓦ visitcopenhagen.com

Money

Denmark is not part of the eurozone, and while some shops will accept euros, Danish kroner (the local currency) is usually preferred. Banks open 10am to 4pm Monday to Wednesday and until 5pm or 5:30 pm Thursday. Most ATMs are open 24/7, and are usually found outside banks and Metro stations. Credit, debit and prepaid currency cards are accepted almost everywhere. Contactless payments are also common. It is the custom to pay cash for transactions under 100Kr. There are many exchange bureaux across the city; those open longest include the **Forex** (8am–9pm) at the central station and the **Danske Bank** exchange office (6am–10pm) at the airport.

Electrical Appliances

You can use your electric appliances in Denmark if the standard voltage in your country is in the range of 220–240 volts. If it is in the range of 100–127 volts (as in the US, Canada and most South American countries), you will need a voltage converter. Sockets take standard European double round-pin plugs, so you may also need to use a plug adaptor.

Mobile Phones and Wi-Fi

GSM-compatible mobile phones work in Denmark, and 4G network coverage is excellent in most of the city. Danish SIM cards can only be bought by Danish residents with a Danish Security Number, but pay-as-you-go cards are available for tourists. The main service providers are **TDC**, **Telenor** and **Telia**. Visitors from the EU can use up to 15GB of their data allowance without being charged an additional fee. Most hotels offer internet access and Wi-Fi. Many trains and buses and some public spaces have free Wi-Fi.

Postal Services

Post offices are open from 9 or 10am to 5:30pm Monday to Friday and 9am to noon on Saturdays. Among the most convenient branches are **Posthus Pilestræde** in the city centre and **Posthus Østerbro** in Østerbro. International mail arrives faster with the Prioritaire mail or Faste Deliver A-mail service, but this can be expensive. Check the **PostNord** website for current rates.

Weather

Denmark has a rather temperate climate, with no extremes of heat or cold, but the weather can be very changeable. July and August are the two hottest and sunniest months in Copenhagen, with temperatures of 19° C (68° F), while the months of January and February are the coldest, with temperatures of 2° C (35° F). The best times to visit are the summer, when you can enjoy as many as 16–18 hours of daylight on clear days, and Christmas, which is when the concept of *hygge* (cosiness) really comes into its own. The only time you might want to avoid visiting – due to chilly winds and limited daylight hours (just 7) – is January.

Opening Hours

Shops are open 9:30 or 10am to 5:30pm Monday to Thursday, 9:30 or 10am to 7 or 8pm Friday and 9:30 or 10am to 3pm Saturday (to 5pm on the first Saturday of the month). Since trading laws have been relaxed, larger shops now open on Sundays. You may find weekend hours extended in tourist areas, especially during summer. Most restaurants will open for dinner at around 6pm, with kitchens typically closing at around 10 or 10:30pm. Booking is always strongly advised, especially if you plan on dining out on Friday and Saturday evenings.

The COVID-19 pandemic proved that situations can change suddenly. Always check before visiting attractions and hospitality venues for up-to-date hours and booking requirements.

Visitor Information

The **Visit Copenhagen** (see p111) tourist office is close to the central railway station and offers visitor information, as well as hotel bookings, car hire, the **Copenhagen Card** and information on tours. Both Copenhagen Card and **Copenhagen City Pass** can be downloaded onto your smartphone and include free admission to some of the top attractions. The *Copenhagen Post* lists all the arts, music and cultural events taking place across the city, while Danish-speakers can check the Friday guide sections of daily newspapers *Politiken* and *Berlingske*. Websites such as **Visit Denmark**, **Copenhagen Tourist** and Visit Copenhagen have plenty of information.

Local Customs

Danes are genuinely friendly and frankly outspoken. It's sensible to brush up on the rules of the road – whether a cyclist, driver or pedestrian – before your arrival. Make eye contact when raising a glass for a toast, and remember hat this is a progressive country, where women's and LGBTQ+ rights are ubiquitous.

Denmark does not have any dress codes for visiting its churches, but be sure to show respect.

Sustainable Travel

Ambitious Copenhagen aims to be carbon neutral in the near future. Play your part by following the lead of the locals and cycling or taking public transport wherever possible, making use of the city's numerous recycling and rubbish bins, and carrying a resuable water bottle. The Visit Copenhagen website also has plenty of advice on how to enjoy the city sustainably, including lists of eco-friendly hotels and shops.

Language

Danish is the only official language of Denmark. An estimated 86 per cent of all Danes speak English as a second language.

Taxes and Refunds

Travellers returning to countries outside the EU are eligible for VAT refunds, though only a limited number of shops in the main cities operate the scheme. Shoppers must spend a minimum of 300Kr per day in the same shop and get a VAT refund certificate at time of purchase. Goods must be presented to customs at the departure point. Refunds are operated by **Premier Tax Free**.

Accommodation

Copenhagen has a wide range of accommodation available, but be aware that it does not come cheap. Make sure you do your research and book well in advance. Weekend stays in hotels can be cheaper than weekdays. If money is not an issue, you'll find plenty of high-end hotels scattered across the city, the most exclusive being the popular five-star Hotel d'Angleterre *(see p114)*, which enjoys a prime location on Kongens Nytorv and features its own in-house spa.

An alternative option is to rent an apartment via **Airbnb** – you'll find many across the city. **Couchsurfing** is another popular way of meeting locals and staying in the city without spending a lot of money.

Places to Stay

PRICE CATEGORIES
For a standard double room per night (with breakfast if included), taxes and extra charges.

Ⓚ under 1,000 ⒦Ⓚ 1,000–2,000 ⒦⒦Ⓚ over 2,000

Luxury Hotels

Copenhagen Plaza
MAP G5 ▪ Bernstorffsgade 4 ▪ 28 30 58 61 ▪ www.ligula.se/profilhotels/copenhagen-plaza ▪ ⒦⒦Ⓚ
Built in 1913, this historic hotel has spacious rooms and traditional decor. The Library Bar is packed with 18th-century books and is among the city's best spots for a nightcap.

Hotel d'Angleterre
MAP K4 ▪ Kongens Nytorv 34 ▪ 33 12 00 95 ▪ www.dangleterre.dk ▪ ⒦⒦Ⓚ
Grandeur meets modern luxury at this hotel. It has a plush palm court, banquet rooms, a spa and an elegant restaurant.

Hotel Front
MAP L4 ▪ Skt Annæ Plads 21 ▪ 33 13 34 00 ▪ www.scandichotels.dk/front ▪ ⒦⒦Ⓚ
Child-friendly hotels can be hard to come by, but this place offers rooms of various sizes. Each room has been uniquely decorated to embrace a cosy and residential feeling.

Manon Les Suites
MAP G4
▪ Gyldenløvesgade 19 ▪ 45 70 00 15 ▪ www.guldsmedenhotels.com/manon-les-suites ▪ ⒦⒦Ⓚ
Manon offers 82 suites, each ideal for a family or five people. The hotel emphasizes sustainability, from daily operations to organic food and beauty products. Room decor is distinctly hip with a mid-century modern flavour.

Nimb Hotel
MAP G5
▪ Bernstorffsgade 5 ▪ 88 70 00 00 ▪ www.nimb.dk ▪ ⒦⒦Ⓚ
One of the most exclusive hotels in Copenhagen, Nimb has 38 rooms. Each of the rooms is unique and luxurious, and their features range from open fireplaces to flatscreen TVs. Housed in the landmark Nimb building, the hotel allows guests to enjoy fine views from the charming Nimb Roof, while relaxing at the pool, bar and lounge.

Nyhavn 71
MAP L4 ▪ Nyhavn 71 ▪ 33 43 62 00 ▪ www.71nyhavnhotel.com ▪ ⒦⒦Ⓚ
This charming hotel was once a warehouse built to store goods from ships in the harbour. The area surrounding the hotel is very peaceful even though it is located near the city's popular canal.

Palace Hotel
MAP H5 ▪ Rådhuspladsen 57 ▪ 33 14 40 50 ▪ www.scandichotels.com/palacehotel ▪ ⒦⒦Ⓚ
Rooms at this Victorian hotel are decorated in an English style but have a modern twist. Celebrities such as Judy Garland, Audrey Hepburn and Errol Flynn have added a touch of glamour to the hotel.

Skt. Petri
MAP H4 ▪ Krystalgade 22 ▪ 33 45 91 00 ▪ www.sktpetri.com ▪ ⒦⒦Ⓚ
Set in Copenhagen's Latin Quarter, this modern hotel housed in a historic building has two restaurants and a bar. There's also a garden courtyard and a fitness studio.

Boutique Hotels

Axel Guldsmeden
MAP G6
▪ Colbjørnsensgade 14 ▪ 33 31 32 66 ▪ www.guldsmedenhotels.com ▪ ⒦Ⓚ
This boutique eco-hotel is close to the main train station. Relax in the saunas and steam baths of the hotel spa and enjoy organic breakfasts in the heated courtyard.

Carlton 66 Guldsmeden
MAP C5 ▪ Vesterbrogade 66 ▪ 33 22 15 00 ▪ www.hotelguldsmeden.dk ▪ ⒦Ⓚ
Sophisticated yet relaxed, this hotel has great decor with dark-wood furniture and Egyptian cotton sheets. Breakfasts are organic.

Hotel Ottilia
MAP B6 ▪ Bryggernes Plads 7 ▪ 33 38 70 30 ▪ www.brochner-hotels.com ▪ ⒦Ⓚ
A true Danish icon that was formerly known as

the Old Carlsberg Brewery, Ottilia has three rooftop restaurants where you get a great view of the city. It is located right next to the famous Elephant Gate in Carlsberg Byen.

Hotel SP34

MAP G4 ■ Sankt Peders Stræde 34 ■ 33 13 30 00 ■ www.brochner-hotels.com ■ Ⓚ Ⓚ
Located in the Latin Quarter, this stylish boutique hotel is not far from Rådhuspladsen. There are 118 beautifully furnished rooms to choose from, all with free Wi-Fi and cable TV. The hotel has two good restaurants, a lounge bar, a café as well as a terrace.

Hotel Twentyseven

MAP H5 ■ Løngangstræde 27 ■ 70 27 56 27 ■ www.firsthotels.com ■ Ⓚ Ⓚ
A boutique hotel with minimalist decor, Hotel Twentyseven is just three minutes from City hall and is not very far from Rådhuspladsen and Strøget. The hotel bars include a wine bar, a cocktail lounge and the Icebar Copenhagen. Guests can also enjoy the daily breakfast buffet.

Imperial Hotel

MAP G5 ■ Vester Farimagsgade 9 ■ 33 12 80 00 ■ www.imperial hotel.dk ■ Ⓚ Ⓚ
Stylish and welcoming, this four-star hotel has been decorated in modern Danish design and has an entire floor dedicated to the work of late Danish designer Børge Mogensen. Allergy-free bedding and non-smoking rooms are available.

Babette Guldsmeden

MAP L2 ■ Bredgade 78 ■ 33 14 15 00 ■ www.guldsmedenhotels.com ■ Ⓚ Ⓚ Ⓚ
Located close to the green area of Kastellet (see p80), this green-certified hotel is inside a 19th-century building. Services include free organic coffee and a full service restaurant.

Hotel Alexandra

MAP G5 ■ H C Andersens Boulevard 8 ■ 33 74 44 44 ■ www.hotelalexandra.dk ■ Ⓚ Ⓚ Ⓚ
This excellent hotel has been around for more than a century and is known for its furniture from the 1950s to 1970s, with design classics ranging from Kaare Klint chairs to Akademi chandeliers designed by artist Poul Henningsen. All second floor rooms are no-smoking and are safe for those with allergies.

Hotel Sanders

MAP K4 ■ Tordenskjoldsgade 15 ■ 46 40 00 40 ■ www.hotelsanders.com ■ Ⓚ Ⓚ
Housed in a Jugendstil building from the 1860s, this boutique hotel's magnificent interior features bespoke furniture and Danish classic design.

Mid-Range Hotels

First Hotel Mayfair

MAP G6 ■ Helgolandsgade 3 ■ 70 12 17 00 ■ www.firsthotels.com ■ Ⓚ Ⓚ
Close to the city's main attractions, this hotel is furnished mainly in an English style with a hint of Asian design.

Ibsens Hotel

MAP G3 ■ Vendersgade 23 ■ 33 13 19 13 ■ www.arthurhotels.dk/ibsens-hotel ■ Ⓚ Ⓚ
With rooms decorated in modern Scandinavian style, this hotel in the Nansensgade area is located a short walk away from Nørreport station and the food market.

The Square

MAP H5 ■ Rådhuspladsen 14 ■ 33 38 12 00 ■ www.thesquarecopenhagen.com ■ Ⓚ Ⓚ
At this three-star hotel is located on the Town Hall square, you will find stylish pony-hair chairs at the entrance and Arne Jacobsen chairs in the reception area. The breakfast is excellent.

Tivoli Hotel

MAP D6 ■ Arni Magnussons Gade 2 ■ 32 68 40 00 ■ www.tivolihotel.com ■ Ⓚ Ⓚ
This high-rise offers activities for kids, as well as a pool and fitness centre. Enjoy lunch or dinner at one of the three restaurants at the hotel. Part of the Tivoli Congress Center, it caters for business guests as well.

Savoy

MAP C5 ■ Vesterbrogade 34 ■ 33 26 75 00 ■ www.savoyhotel.dk ■ Ⓚ Ⓚ
Dating from 1906, this 66-room hotel is known for its distinctive Art Nouveau façade, and is a Vesterbro landmark. Renovated but still affordable, it has Wi-Fi in all rooms and a guest PC in the lobby. The rooms facing the courtyard are much quieter.

Rooms with a View

Danhostel Copenhagen City

MAP J6 ▪ H C Andersens Blvd 50 ▪ 33 11 85 85 ▪ www.danhostel copenhagencity.dk ▪ Ⓚ

This modern and design-led Danhostel is one of the biggest in the city. It is located close to Tivoli and Rådhuspladsen.

Dragør Badehotel

MAP C3 ▪ Drogdensvej 43, Dragør ▪ 32 53 05 00 ▪ www.badehotellet.dk ▪ Ⓚ

The fishing village of Dragør is popular with tourists and this hotel's rooms have good views of the sea and countryside.

Copenhagen Island

MAP J6 ▪ Kalvebod Brygge 53 ▪ 33 38 96 00 ▪ www.copenhagen island.com ▪ ⓀⓀⓀ

This state-of-the-art hotel is located on an island in the middle of Copenhagen harbour. Designed by architect, Kim Utzon, this extra-ordinary building places a great emphasis on the play of light when it comes in contact with glass. The rooms offer scenic views of the Sound. It also has its own, very well-equipped gym and fitness centre.

Copenhagen Strand

MAP L4 ▪ Havnegade 37 ▪ 33 48 99 00 ▪ www.copenhagenstrand.com ▪ ⓀⓀ

With a rustic decor, this three-star hotel is housed in a 1869 harbourfront warehouse that is tucked away on a pretty, quiet street opposite the Christianshavns canal.

Kurhotel Skodsborg

MAP B2 ▪ Skodsborg Strandvej 139, Skodsborg ▪ 45 58 58 00 ▪ www.skodsborg.dk ▪ ⓀⓀ

Once a summer palace, this century-old health resort is a lovely place to stay. Set in a countryside and overlooking the sea, the hotel offers a good range of therapies, fitness programmes, a relaxing spa and healthy food.

Skovshoved Hotel

MAP B2 ▪ Strandvejen 267, Charlottenlund ▪ 39 64 00 28 ▪ www.skovshovedhotel.com ▪ ⓀⓀ

Away from the bustle of central Copenhagen, this elegant seaside hotel is more than 350 years old. Tastefully decorated in a Scandinavian style, it is surrounded by fishermen's houses and offers beautiful views. Be sure to book ahead as this restaurant is listed in the Michelin Guide.

Admiral

MAP L3 ▪ Toldbodgade 24–28 ▪ 33 74 14 14 ▪ www.admiralhotel.dk ▪ ⓀⓀⓀ

Originally an 18th-century granary, this four-star hotel in the city centre is within easy reach of shopping areas, theatres and other attractions. Its rooms have stunning views of the Operaen (see pp94–5). The foyer has models of ships. The restaurant, Salt, is excellent.

Hotel CPHLIVING

MAP J6 ▪ Langebrogade 1A ▪ 61 60 85 46 ▪ www.cphliving.com ▪ ⓀⓀⓀ

Copenhagen's first floating hotel is built on a barge and located in the inner harbour in the centre of the city. There are 12 rooms, all with views of the old town and harbour.

Radisson Collection Royal Hotel, Copenhagen

MAP G5 ▪ Hammerichsgade 1 ▪ 33 42 60 00 ▪ www.radisson.com ▪ ⓀⓀⓀ

This famous Radisson hotel, designed by Arne Jacobsen in the 1950s, is packed with five-star comforts. The rooms have great views. Café Royal on the 20th floor serves high-end cuisine and afternoon tea.

Budget Hotels

CabInn City

MAP H6 ▪ Mitchellsgade 14 ▪ 33 46 16 16 ▪ www.cabinn.com ▪ Ⓚ

Based on the idea of a ship's cabin, the rooms at CabInn City are cozy with all the modern conveniences tucked into a clever storage design. You can pick from bunk beds in twin rooms, double rooms and family rooms. The hotel has a pleasant ambience and every morning there is a good buffet breakfast.

CabInn Metro

MAP H6 ▪ Arne Jakobsens Allé 2 ▪ 32 46 57 00 ▪ www.cabinn.com ▪ Ⓚ

The Metro, Denmark's largest hotel, is the fourth hotel in the city's budget CabInn concept. It is located very close to the city's airport and Field's shopping centre. All of the rooms are modern, clean, and all have en-suite facilities. The conference centre can seat upto 65 people.

CabInn Scandinavia
MAP C4 ■ Vodroffsvej 55, Frederiksberg ■ 35 36 11 11 ■ www.cabinn. com ■ ⓚ

This CabInn hotel is just a block away from the CabInn Express and a road before the Peblinge Lake. It is equipped with all the modern conveniences found at the other three CabInns in the city.

Generator Hostel Copenhagen
MAP K3 ■ Adelgade 5–7 ■ 78 77 54 00 ■ www. generatorhostels.com ■ ⓚ

A smart, modern hostel with private, en-suite rooms as well as dorms. Facilities include Wi-Fi, a bar and breakfast (for an extra charge).

Hotel Copenhagen
MAP E6 ■ Egilsgade 33, Islands Brygge ■ 32 96 27 27 ■ www.hotel copenhagen.dk ■ ⓚ

Just a few minutes away from the city centre by Metro, this hotel offers rooms that can sleep up to four and have shared bathrooms. There are also some very nice rooms with en-suite facilities. Free Wi-Fi is available in the reception and, for a small charge, a breakfast can be ordered when you book.

Wakeup Copenhagen Carsten Niebuhrs Gade
MAP D6 ■ Carsten Niebuhrs Gade 11 ■ 44 80 00 10 ■ www.wakeup copenhagen.dk ■ ⓚ

Designed by architect Kim Utzon, this ultramodern, two-star budget hotel is located along the waterfront, close to Fisketorvet shopping mall. It is minimally decorated and all the rooms are equipped with modern amenities.

Wakeup Copenhagen Borgergade
MAP K3 ■ Borgergade 9 ■ 44 80 00 90 ■ www. wakeupcopenhagen.dk ■ ⓚⓚ

This 498-room hotel offers ultramodern accommodation just minutes from Kongens Nytorv, Amalienborg and other city-centre sights. The interior is extremely stylish and part of a new generation of budget accommodation appearing in the city.

Hostels and Apartments

Copenhagen Downtown Hostel
MAP J5 ■ Vandkunsten 5 ■ 70 23 21 10 ■ www. copenhagendowntown. com ■ ⓚ

Located in the heart of the city, this hostel promises a vibrant, artistic as well as international atmosphere. It has a café, lounge as well as a restaurant. In addition to the dorm and four-bedded rooms, there are rooms with en-suite facilities for two to three people. A YHA membership card is required, but this can also be purchased while checking in.

DCU-Copenhagen Camp "Absalon" UK
Korsdalsvej 132, DK-2610 Rødovre ■ 36 41 06 00 ■ www.dcu.dk ■ ⓚ

Visitors can park their caravans here or sleep in tents. There are also 45 cabins, most with en-suite facilities. There are recreational areas including a playground with bouncing cushions and chess here. Guests also get access to Wi-Fi.

Steel House Copenhagen
MAP C5 ■ Herholdtsgade 6 ■ 33 17 71 10 ■ www. steelhousecopenhagen. com ■ ⓚ

This 253-room hostel, which opened in the summer of 2017, is a stone's throw from the Vesterport Station. Sleek rooms range from 6- and 4-bed dorms to single rooms. In addition to a self-service kitchen and cool craft-beer bar, there are sports facilities, a café, reading lounge, business centre, pool and music venue.

STAY Kastellet
MAP F3 ■ Indiakaj 14 ■ 72 44 44 34 ■ www. stayapartments.dk/ kastellet ■ ⓚⓚⓚ

Visitors can choose from 23 spacious apartments with fully furnished rooms and equipped kitchens. This hotel is located close to Østerport station and is just around the corner from the Little Mermaid.

STAY Seaport
MAP F1 ■ Murmanskgade 15 ■ 72 44 44 34 ■ https:// stayapartments.dk/ seaport ■ ⓚⓚⓚ

With breathtaking views of the Copenhagen harbour and Øresund from the rooftop, STAY Seaport offers spacious apartments furnished with high-end, branded amenities. There are fully equipped kitchens as well as a modern in-house gym.

General Index

Acknowledgments

This edition updated by

Contributor Allan Mutuku-Kortbæk
Senior Editor Alison McGill
Senior Designer Stuti Tiwari
Project Editors Dipika Dasgupta, Lucy Sara-Kelly
Project Art Editor Ankita Sharma
Assistant Editors Priya Bhowal, Anjasi N.N.
Picture Research Administrator Vagisha Pushp
Picture Research Manager Taiyaba Khatoon
Publishing Assistant Halima Mohammed
Jacket Designer Jordan Lambley
Senior Cartographer Mohammed Hassan
Cartography Manager Suresh Kumar
DTP Designer Rohit Rojal
Senior Production Editor Jason Little
Production Controller Samantha Cross
Deputy Managing Editor Beverly Smart
Managing Editors Shikha Kulkarni, Hollie Teague
Managing Art Editor Sarah Snelling
Senior Managing Art Editor Priyanka Thakur
Art Director Maxine Pedliham
Publishing Director Georgina Dee

DK would like to thank the following for their contribution to the previous editions: Antonia Cunningham, Chris Moss, Hilary Bird.

Nationalmuseet, Danmark: Roberto Fortuna and Kira Ursem 11clb, 33br; Lennart Larsen 32br; John Lee 33tr.

Normann Copenhagen: Jeppe Sørensen 81tr.

North Atlantic House: 94tr.

Ny Carlsberg Glyptotek: Ana Cecilia Gonzalez 2tr, 34–5; Kim Nilsson 44b.

Orangeriet Kongens Have: 83cla.

Ordrupgaard: Anders Sune Berg 99br.

Radisson Collection Royal Hotel, Copenhagen: 88b.

Ripley Entertainment Inc: Copenhagen Guinness World Records Museum / Johanne Lerbech 52bl.

Royal Copenhagen Porcelain: Gab Admin 73cb.

The Royal Danish Theatre: Christophe Pelç 54b; Costin Radu 23crb; Egon Street 95cl.

Rust: 82b.

SMK – National Gallery of Denmark: 11cra, 26cla, 26br, 27tr, 45cl, 79cl.

SuperStock: Yadid Levy 73cra.

Shutterstock.com: Yuliya Ivanenko 49cla, Dan Race 93b.

Team Bade / Islands Brygge Harbour Bath: 13tl, 49tr.

The Danish Jewish Museum: 31tl; Josefine Amalie 44tl.

The Royal Danish Collection: 24cra; Iben Bolling Kaufmann 10crb, 16crb, 43br; Peter Norby 16–17, 17tl; Peter Nørby 11tl, 25crb, 25br.

Tivoli: Anders Bøggild 10c, 52t; Rasmus B. Hansen 15tl; Lasse Salling 14cla, 14bl, 14–15, 15br.

The Viking Ship Museum, Denmark: Werner Karrasch 99t, 102cla.

WarPigs Brewpub: Camilla Stephan & Rasmus Malmstr 57tr.

Cover

Front and spine: Alamy Stock Photo: Kavalenkava Volha.

Back: Dreamstime.com: Arndale crb; Belier tl; Scanrail cla; **Getty Images:** Alexander Spatari; **Alamy Stock Photo:** Kavalenkava Volha b.

Pull Out Map Cover

Alamy Stock Photo: Kavalenkava Volha.

All other images © Dorling Kindersley
For further information see:
www.dkimages.com

Penguin Random House

First edition 2007

Published in Great Britain by
Dorling Kindersley Limited
DK, One Embassy Gardens, 8 Viaduct Gardens, London SW11 7BW, UK

The authorised representative in the EEA is
Dorling Kindersley Verlag GmbH. Arnulfstr.
124, 80636 Munich, Germany

Published in the United States by
DK Publishing, 1745 Broadway, 20th Floor,
New York, NY 10019, USA

Copyright © 2007, 2023 Dorling Kindersley Limited

A Penguin Random House Company

23 24 25 26 10 9 8 7 6 5 4 3 2 1

A CIP catalogue record is available from the British Library.

A catalogue record for this book is available from the Library of Congress.

ISSN 1479-344X

ISBN 978-0-2416-1865-3

Printed and bound in Malaysia

www.dk.com

As a guide to abbreviations in visitor information blocks: **Adm** = admission charge; **D** = dinner; **L** = lunch.

Phrase Book

In an Emergency

Help!	Hjælp!	yellb!
Stop!	Stands!	stanns!
Can you call a doctor?	Kan du ringe til en læge?	kann do ringe-til ehn laiyeh?
Can you call an ambulance?	Kan du ringe til en ambulance?	kann do ringe-til ehn ahm-boo-lang-seh?
Can you call the police?	Kan du ringe til politiet?	kann do ringe-til po-ly-tee'd?
Can you call the fire brigade?	Kan du ringe til brand-væsenet?	kann do ringe-til brahn-vaiys-ned?
Is there a telephone here?	Er der en telefon i nærheden?	e-ah dah ehn tele-fohn ee neya-hethen?
Where is the nearest hospital?	Hvor er det nærmeste hospital?	voa e-ah deh neh-meste hoh-spee-tahl

Useful Phrases

Sorry	Undskyld	ons-gull
Goodnight	Godnat	goh-nad
Goodbye	Farvel	fah-vell
Good evening	Godaften	goh-ahf-tehn
Good morning	Godmorgen	goh-moh'n
Good day (after about 9am)	Goddag	goh-dah
Yes	Ja	yah
No	Nej	nye
Please	Værsgo/Velbekomme	vehs-goh/vell-beh-commeh
Thank you	Tak	tahgg
How are you?	Hvordan har du det?/Hvordan går det?	voh-dann hah do deh?/voh-dan go deh?
Well, thank you	Godt, tak	gohd, tahgg
Pleased to have met you	Det var rart at møde dig	deh vah rahd add meutheh die
See you!	Vi ses!	vee sehs!
I understand	Jeg forstår	yay fuh-stoah
I don't understand	Jeg forstår ikke	yay fuh-stoah egge
Does anyone speak English?	Er der nogen, der kan tale engelsk?	e-ah dah noh-enn dah kann tah-leh eng-ellsgg?
good	god	guth
bad	dårlig	doh-lee
up	op	ohb
down	ned	neth
near	tæt på	taid poh
far	langt fra	lahngd fra
on the left	til venstre	till vehn-streh
on the right	til højre	till hoy-reh
open	åben	oh-ben
closed	lukket	luh-geth
warm	varm	vahm
cold	kold	koll
big	stor	stoah
little	lille	lee-leh

Making a Telephone Call

Whom am I speaking to?	Hvem taler jeg med?	vemm talah yay meth?
I would like to call…	Jeg vil gerne ringe til…	yay vill geh-neh ring-eh till…
I will telephone again	Jeg ringer en gang til	yay ring-ah ehn gahng till

In a Hotel

Do you have double rooms?	Findes her dobbelt-værelser?	feh-ness he-ah dob-belld vah-hel-sah?
With bathroom	Med bade-værelse	meth bah-the-vah-hel-sah
With washbasin	Med hånd-vask	meth hohn-vasgg
key	nøgle	noy-leh
I have a reservation	Jeg har en reservation	yay hah ehn res-sah-vah-shohn

Sightseeing

entrance	indgang	ehn-gahng
exit	udgang	ooth-gahng
exhibition	udstilling	ooth-stelling
tourist information	turisto-plysning	tooh-reesd-ohb-lehs-ning
town/city hall	rådhus	rahd-hus
post office	posthus	posd-hus
cathedral	domkirke	dom-kia-keh
church	kirke	kia-keh
museum	museum	muh-seh-uhm
town bus	bybus	bih-boos
long-distance bus	rutebil	bus roo-teh-beel
railway station	banegård	bah-neh-goh
airport	lufthavn	luhft-havn
train	tog	toh
ferry terminal	færgehavn	fah-veh-havn
bus stop	busstoppested	buhs-sdob-beh-steth
long-distance bus station	rutebilstation	roo-teh-beel-sta-shion
a public toilet	et offentligt toilet	ehd off-end-ligd toa-led

Shopping

I wish to buy…	Jeg vil gerne købe…	yay vill geh-neh kyh-beh…
Do you have…?	Findes der…?	feh-ness de-ah…?
How much does it cost?	Hvad koster det?	vath koh-stah deh
expensive	dyr	dyh-ah
cheap	billig	billy
size	størrelse	stoh-ell-seh
general store	købmand	keuhb-mann
greengrocer	grønthandler	grund-handla
supermarket	supermarked	suh-pah-mah-keth
market	marked	mah-keth

Eating Out

Do you have a table for… people?	Har I et bord til… personer?	hah ee ed boah till… peh-soh-nah?
I would like to sit by the window	Jeg vil gerne sidde ved vinduet	yay vill geh-neh saithe veth veen-do-ed

I wish to order...	**Jeg vil gerne bestille...**	yay vill geh-neh beh-stilleh...
I'm a vegetarian	**Jeg er vegetar**	yay eh-ah veh-gehta
children's menu	**børnemenu**	byeh-neh-meh-nye
daily special	**dagens ret**	dayens rad
starter	**forret**	foh-red
main course	**hovedret**	hoh-veth-red
dessert	**dessert**	deh-seh'd
wine list	**vinkort**	veen-cod
sweet	**sødt**	sodt
sour	**surt**	suad
spicy	**stærkt**	stehgd
May I have the bill?	**Må jeg bede om regningen?**	moh yay beh-theh uhm rahy-ning-ehn

Menu Decoder

agurk	a-guag	cucumber
ananas	a-nah-nas	pineapple
appelsin	abbel-seen	orange
blomme	blum-ma	plum
brød	bruth	bread
champignon	sham-pee-ong	mushroom
danskvand	dansg vann	mineral water
fersken	fes-gehn	peach
fisk	fesgg	fish
fløde	flu-theh	cream
gulerod	gooleh-roth	carrot
grøntsager	grunn-saha	vegetables
hummer	humma	lobster
is	ees	ice cream
kaffe	kah-feh	coffee
kartofler	kah-toff-lah	potatoes
kød	kuth	meat
kylling	killing	chicken
kål	kohl	cabbage
laks	lahggs	salmon
lam	lahm	lamb
leverpostej	leh-vah-poh-stie	liver paté
løg	loy	onion
mælk	mailgg	milk
oksekød	ogg-seh-kuth	beef
ost	ossd	cheese
peber	peh-ba	pepper
pore	po-a	leek
purløj	poo-a-loy	chives
pølse	pill-seh	sausage
rejer	rah-yah	shrimps
ris	rees	rice
rødspætte	roth-speh-da	plaice
røget fisk	roy-heth fesgg	smoked fish
saftevand	sah-fteh-vann	squash
salat	sah-lad	salad
salt	sald	salt
sild	sil	herring
skaldyr	sgall-dya	shellfish
skinke	sgeng-geh	ham
smør	smuah	butter
sodavand	sodah-vann	fizzy drink
steg	stie	steak
svinekød	svee-neh-kuth	pork
syltetøj	sill-teh-toi	jam
te	teh	tea
tærte	te-ah-teh	quiche/pie
torsk	tohsgg	cod
vand	vann	water
wienerbrød	vee-nah-bryd	Danish pastry
æble	eh-bleh	apple
æg	egg	egg
øl	uhl	beer

Time

today	**i dag**	ee-day
tomorrow	**i morgen**	ee-mohn
yesterday	**i går**	ee-goh
before noon	**formiddag**	foh-medday
afternoon	**eftermiddag**	ehftah-medday
evening	**aften**	ahftehn
night	**nat**	nadd
minute	**minut**	meh-nude
hour	**time**	tee-meh
week	**uge**	oo-eh
month	**måned**	moe-neth
year	**år**	oah

Days of the Week

Monday	**mandag**	mann-day
Tuesday	**tirsdag**	teahs-day
Wednesday	**onsdag**	uns-day
Thursday	**torsdag**	toahs-day
Friday	**fredag**	frey-day
Saturday	**lørdag**	lur-day
Sunday	**søndag**	son-day

Months

January	**januar**	ya-nuah
February	**februar**	fib-buah
March	**marts**	mahds
April	**april**	apreal
May	**maj**	mai
June	**juni**	yoo-nee
July	**juli**	yoo-lee
August	**august**	auw-guhsd
September	**september**	sehb-tem-bah
October	**oktober**	ogg-toh-bah
November	**november**	noh-vem-bah
December	**december**	deh-sem-bah

Numbers

0	**nul**	noll
1	**en**	ehn
2	**to**	toh
3	**tre**	tray
4	**fire**	fee-ah
5	**fem**	femm
6	**seks**	seggs
7	**syv**	siu
8	**otte**	oh-deh
9	**ni**	nee
10	**ti**	tee
20	**tyve**	tyh-veh
30	**tredive**	traith-veh
40	**fyrre**	fyr-reh
50	**halvtreds**	hahl-traiths
60	**tres**	traiths
70	**halvfjerds**	hahl-fyads
80	**firs**	fee-ahs
90	**halvfems**	hahl-femms
100	**hundrede**	hoon-dreh-the
200	**tohundrede**	toh-hoon-dreh-the
1,000	**tusind**	tooh-sin-deh
2,000	**totusinde**	toh-tooh-sin-deh

Selected Copenhagen Street Index